To Gor

Arthur

6th March 1993.

THE STORY OF TIM

THE STORY OF TIM

ARTHUR STOCKWIN

Paul Norbury Publications
Sandgate, Folkestone, Kent, England

THE STORY OF TIM

First published 1993
by Paul Norbury Publications
Knoll House, 35 The Crescent
Sandgate, Folkestone, Kent CT20 3EE

*Paul Norbury Publications is an imprint of
Curzon Press Ltd — St John's Studios, Church Road,
Richmond, Surrey TW9 2QA*

© 1993 Arthur Stockwin

All rights reserved.
No part of this publication may be reproduced or transmitted
in any form or by any means without written permission
from the publishers.

British Library Cataloguing in Publication Data
A CIP catalogue entry for this book
is available from the British Library

ISBN 1-873410-20-4

Set in Plantin 11 on 12½ point by Visual Typesetting, Harrow, Middlesex
Keywork by Ann Tiltman

Printed in Great Britain by BPCC Wheatons Ltd, Exeter

*for all who knew Tim
and all who have lost children*

Table of Contents

	Preface	ix
1	Australia	1
2	Becoming Australian	7
3	Interlude in Britain	13
4	Interlude in Japan	23
5	Growing up in Australia (I)	33
6	Growing up in Australia (II)	38
7	Changing Country	48
8	Trying not to be English	56
9	Pond Life, Drums, Drama and Village Cricket	65
10	A Change of Education	77
11	The Yellow Bullet	85
12	Oxford Entrance	92
13	Race Relations in East Oxford, Landscape in Yorkshire	101
14	The Heights of Cricket	105
15	Zimbabwe	114
16	Dairy and Bicycles	122
17	Europe-Interrail	125
18	One of Life's Little Things	136
19	Mega-Party	140
20	Austria	143
	Epilogue	148
	Poems	157

Preface

Sons write biographies of their famous fathers, but how often do fathers write biographies of their sons? Sons and daughters are part of the furniture of our lives - loved, loving, irritated, irritating, sometimes noticed more, sometimes less, using home as a haven and parents as a sounding board, rebelling, adjusting, developing, but always somehow in communion with that evolutionary structure of parents and children and associated others known as the family.

As father of four children, the idea never remotely entered my head that I should attempt a biography of any of them. At times I idly compared my own and my wife's childhood with theirs, so different yet with points in common, and I wondered why it was that the four of them were diverging as much from each other as from their parents in their interests and approaches to life, and yet as a family we were all close and had much in common. And then one evening in late December 1987, two days before Christmas, we learned that Tim, the youngest, had died on a ski slope in Austria. He was just three days past his nineteenth birthday.

In the weeks and months after that bewildering night, when we realised that we had been buying Christmas presents for him in the afternoon when he was already dead, I learned much about Tim that I had not known or known only imperfectly from his friends, his schoolteachers and others. I knew that he was adventurous, sports-mad and a hugely talented cricketer, that he was gregarious and could relate to most types of people, that he enjoyed riotous behaviour with his mates in the pub, but also read poetry and was deeply serious about issues of social inequality. I realised that he was ambitious and intended to do well, but also that he had a critical, even rebellious streak, and that he was politically more left wing than most of his friends. What I had not fully realised was the depth of loyalty that he inspired among many who knew him, the ability to manage people displayed as cricket captain, the sheer speed at which his various talents were developing at the time he died.

To combine the role of father and objective biographer must be no less hard than in the case of a son as biographer of a father. Obviously I am a biased witness. But my intention is to be as objective as I can. Also the book is in no sense meant as a dirge. Tim's life was full of lightness and humour and excitement, and I want to convey that in its full extent. Those who want to read about Tim and his life are advised to finish reading at the end of Chapter 20. I have also written an epilogue which is intended to be of some help to others who may have had to cope with a situation such as we were faced with from the end of 1987.

This book could not have been written without help or inspiration from many people, and in particular our family: Audrey, Kate and Michael, Jane and Russell, Rupert and Maggy, Alice, Eric and Pam, Norman and Kathleen, Mick and Wendy, Ali and Evan, Roy and Ann; Tim's Australian friends Rob and Stephen; his Oxford friends Alison, Andy C., Angus, Anna, Anna Jo, Christian, Jon, Mick M., Nick T., Pete L., Philippa, Rupert S., Stephen W.; Jonathan, who stayed with us during the autumn of 1987, Robert, who corresponded with Tim after they met at the Oxford Entrance exam; from the cricketing world in the Oxford area, Chris Bishop, John Fulkes, Michael Search and Don Slatter; the late Dick Procktor, Headmaster of the Oxford School; Iain Adamson, Ted Adnams and Pat Hall of the Marlborough School, Woodstock; William Cook (the Master), Nigel Bates, Rev. David Dunning, John Harrop, Mike Joyce, Dr Brian Martin, Neil Rollings and Duncan Smith of Magdalen College School, Oxford; in Austria Herr Freisleben, Dr Jeleff and members of the ski patrol at Klösterle; Paul, an Australian who worked with Tim at the Gasthof Freisleben, and Michael, a German who skied with Tim on the final day.

Others who wrote to us about their impressions of Tim or otherwise gave particular support in the writing of it included: Shiro and Yuko Abe, Junji and Kazuko Banno, Carlo and Janice Bonasera, Pat and Archie Brown, John and Jay Buckler, Mary Bull, Margaret Campbell, Jenny Corbett and Andrew

Preface

Schuller, Barbara and Graham Dawson, Diana Dick, Audrey Duke, Ann Gluckman, Jill Hopkins, Mike Howarth, Peter and Margaret Janssens, Martin and Annetta Lawrence, Elizabeth and Kit Liew, Roger and Anne Lonsdale, Mary and Dan Lunn, Jocelyn and Peter Morris, Teresa and Chris Pomfret, Harry and Norma Rigby, Alan and Judy Rix, Peter Sowden, Mieko Sugai, Ann Waswo, Mollie and Ernest Whittemore.

I should also like to express appreciation to the many generous contributors to the Tim Stockwin Memorial Fund.

Tim, summer 1987

1 Australia

In 1968 the Canberra suburb of Aranda was little more than a dusty building site in low rainfall eucalyptus forest (dry sclerophyll forest) on the lower eastern slopes of Black Mountain. It was to be the beginning of a huge new satellite town called Belconnen, stretching from Black Mountain over farming country almost to where the Murrumbidgee River wound through a deep gorge towards its confluence with the Murray many miles downstream. The summer of 1967-8, which we missed because we were away in England, had been the hottest for a generation, and those hardy pioneers who had already bought houses in Aranda and its neighbouring suburb Macquarie, spoke of appalling conditions of dust and heat, with virtually no local services of any kind.

By the time we bought our small box-like single-storey house in one of the lowest parts of Aranda in August 1968, conditions were improving. August in Australia is the middle of winter, and the terrible drought which visited the Southern Tablelands of New South Wales and the Australian Capital Territory in the first six months of that year had already broken. There was heavy frost at night, often brilliant blue skies during the day, but enough rain to lay the yellow and red dust. The wattles - the national flower of Australia - were just about to come into bloom, while crimson rosellas and king parrots flashed startlingly vivid patches of colour amid the olive green of the eucalyptus.

Our neighbours were planning and laying out their gardens, services such as shops and schools were starting up and families were getting to know each other. It was an extraordinarily young community, in which nearly every family consisted of parents in their twenties or early thirties with small children. One evening, after we had lived for some months in Aranda, a Salvation Army band arrived in our road and began playing hymn tunes. Suddenly, a sea of children poured out of their houses and into the road, mesmerised as though by the Pied Piper.

Not only the brand new suburbs of Belconnen, but also Canberra in general, had a population that was young and mobile. This was Australia's federal capital, conceived in the early years of the century because neither Sydney nor Melbourne would agree to the other being the capital, based on the design of the American Walter Burley Griffin who had been a pupil of Frank Lloyd Wright.

Actual construction was begun in the 1920s in the valley of the Molonglo River, a few miles above where it flows into the Murrumbidgee, in an area where sheep farming had taken place since the nineteenth century. The flood plain of the Molonglo was earmarked according to Burley Griffin's plan, for the construction of an artificial lake, which should bisect Australia's capital and provide a unity based on water.

From the early 1930s, however, the development of Canberra languished. Although Parliament moved there in 1927 followed by some Commonwealth (i.e. federal) government departments, first the Great Depression and then the Second World War stopped Canberra in its tracks. The lake was not built, the population in 1950 was a mere 23,000 and it was derided throughout Australia as the 'bush capital', 'the federal village', 'seven suburbs in search of a city' and 'a sheep property spoiled'.

More ominously, many Australians (and some of their politicians) regarded it as a gross waste of taxpayers' money and a device for putting politicians and public servants in a remote place, away from contact with the real concerns of real people. As late as the 1950s there were still those who publicly argued that Canberra should be scrapped completely.

We ourselves had a nasty little illustration of how Canberra tended to be regarded, some time after we arrived in Australia in 1960. We had driven our venerable Morris Minor up from Canberra to Sydney and were staying at a cheap establishment called the People's Palace at the sleazier end of Pitt Street. The car was parked in the street and as we approached it we saw some drunks walk past it and notice the Canberra registration plates. One of them stopped, growled 'Canberra!' and deliberately spat at the car.

If Canberra was unpopular in the rest of Australia, it was hardly a comfortable or convenient place for those who lived there. In the early 1950s people routinely drove 65 miles along the Federal Highway towards Sydney as far as the country town of Goulburn to do any serious shopping beyond buying basic groceries. Bricks were rarely obtainable for private building and most houses had to be built of wood or fibro cement. Bottled milk was not delivered until around 1955; before then householders had to receive milk ladled out of churns. Even though the 'seven suburbs' were widely scattered (and deliberately so, in pursuit of the Burley Griffin plan) on both sides of the non-existent lake, bus services were abysmal. Whenever the Molonglo flooded, two of the three bridges across it would be cut.

Reaching Canberra from anywhere else was apt to be a long, slow process. When we first went to Canberra in March 1960, we took a train from Melbourne to Albury on the Victoria-New South Wales border, where we had to change to another train as the rail gauges were still different in the two States. We left this train at Yass Junction, a tiny halt-like station out of sight of the small town of Yass itself, and took a mini-bus for some 35 miles to Canberra. When we finally arrived at the national capital on a Saturday afternoon, it appeared to be completely deserted. The alternative of travelling to Canberra by train through Goulburn would, we were told, have taken an extra five hours. Canberra had an airport, it is true, but in 1960 the 'terminal' was still a modest wooden building. Since most of the employment was provided by the Commonwealth Government, Canberra had the atmosphere of a company town, only it was the Government that was the 'company'.

When we arrived in Canberra, however, it was already rapidly changing. In 1957 a decision had been made to lift the place out of its stagnation and develop it as a true capital city. The lake would be built, other functions of the government would be brought to Canberra, services and the look of the city would be improved, new population would be attracted, along with the service industries needed to put the place on its feet. A body called the 'National Capital Development Commission' was set up to plan the city's development. During the 1960s and early 1970s Canberra prospered as never before, its population growing at some 10 per cent per year. There were less than 50,000 people in Canberra when we arrived in 1960, but perhaps 200,000 by the mid 1970s. This was also a period of optimism and new ideas in Australia as a whole, in which many things seemed to be possible. It was also, however, a period in which Australia's involvement in the Vietnam war became more and more controversial and ultimately precipitated turmoil and change.

There was a growth of Australian self-confidence and nationalism, a breaking away from 'old country' ties with a Britain whose world role was visibly receding, and a sense of creating a new society from the various ethnic groups of which Australia was now composed. Canberra, though it still suffered from its long history of retarded development, felt itself to be in the vanguard of progressive change. Though some might still look upon it as a federal backwater, or somehow 'unAustralian', many Canberrans felt that this was where decisions were being made that were going to be crucial to the nation's future, and that the planned environment of Canberra itself had a wider relevance. Although it had taken us a long time to get into this frame of mind, Canberra and Australia by the late 1960s seemed an exciting place to live, and the future was challenging.

Tim was born on 20 December 1968 in the maternity ward of the Canberra Community Hospital on a peninsula in Lake Burley Griffin, which had been created some five years before. His sisters, Kate (Katrina) and Jane, and brother Rupert, had all been born in the same hospital in 1961, 1964 and 1966, respectively. By this time their mother, Audrey, was well experienced in the art of childbirth, and in any case Tim's birth was easier than some of the previous ones. In accordance with enlightened, but at the time rather novel, hospital practice, I had been allowed to witness all four births. Tim was a normal healthy baby, distinguished from his red-headed sisters and fair-to-brown-haired brother by hair which was intensely blonde. His brilliant white hair was his trade mark, and remained with him throughout his life, never darkening.

From the hospital it was possible to watch geese and ducks on the lake, as well as various classes of small sailing dinghy. Indeed, one summer in the 1970s, because of the drying-out of watercourses further north, the lake was invaded by a colony of pelicans, huge white birds who with their seaplane landings and takings off entertained the people right in the middle of Australia's capital city. On Christmas Day 1968 I took Kate, Jane and Rupert to meet their new brother. Unusually for mid summer, it was a day of very heavy rain, but in the late afternoon the rain lifted, the hot sun came out, the ground glistened and that magic Australian smell of hot wet earth and eucalyptus vapour pervaded the air. Audrey was 32 years old and I was 33. We had all of the family we had planned. Truly, it was a happy time.

For a few days after release from hospital, Audrey and Tim stayed in a home for mothers and new-born babies. It was quite a small and informal place, with a relaxed Australian efficiency about it. One episode, however, perplexed me greatly, though I also found it amusing and told it on occasion to our friends. It was then still some time before the Americans landed a man on the moon, but on 21 December Apollo 8, with three astronauts on board, circled the moon and photographed the side invisible from earth. This was very hot news at the time, and everybody was talking about it. Indeed, it was part of the general optimism and belief in progress of the 1960s.

Even though the home was an informal kind of place, there was naturally an admission form to fill in (or fill out, as Australians say), and I was ushered into the Matron's office to give details which she could enter on the form. After the normal questions concerning name, occupation etc., there was one which is always awkward, namely 'what is your religion?' I answered 'no religion'. Immediately, I could see I had said the wrong thing. Even though the home was not a religious foundation I realised that the Matron was passionate about her religion and could not cope with someone who wanted her to write 'no religion' on her admission form.

'We believe here', she said, 'that babies are the gift of God'. I did not propose to get into an argument with her and made no significant reply. And then, in an effort to convince me she began talking about the latest Apollo mission, making a comparison between the resurrection of Jesus Christ and the lift-off from earth of the astronauts. Both, apparently, were examples of the same kind of phenomenon, whereby God acted to liberate individuals from earth's gravity. So far as the form was concerned, she refused to accept 'no religion' and insisted on writing that the religion of our family was 'humanist'. I did not like being described as anything with 'ist' on the end, but was so bemused by the attitudes I was encountering that I let it pass without argument.

I had, of course, met this kind of strange world view before, but not in somebody who had received scientific and administrative training at a level needed to run a medical establishment. It set me wondering whether truth was in some way more relative than I had assumed. Was I being in some way arrogant in mentally dismissing what I had heard as unscientific? I thought not: however I looked at it, that seemed exactly how it should be described. And yet this was part of the broader problem about how one's assumptions about the world can be validated. I had done some philosophy as an undergraduate and knew that this was the stuff of much philosophical debate. Years later, when Tim was in his later years of secondary schooling and becoming intellectually aware, I could see that he too was having to confront basic questions about his own orientation towards reality, and that he was doing this not only through study and reading, but through other interests such as music, sport and arguing about politics, and through his sheer joy in interacting with other people.

Of course, at the time we are talking about, Tim was far away from such concerns. Finding enough milk and settling his stomach were no doubt his prime interests in the first days and weeks of life. When he was brought home to our house in Aranda in time for the New Year of 1969, he was the centre of attention and had several pairs of hands to help look after him, under Audrey's watchful eye.

2 Becoming Australian

Our house in Aranda, which we bought at what now seems a rock-bottom price (although it didn't then) with the help of a fixed-interest university loan, was a simple three-bedroom single-storey spec-built box. It had an open plan kitchen/dining room divided by a bench for eating breakfast, and a living room at the front of the house with a big window facing the road some distance away. The bathroom included a tiled shower which, unlike any we ever met in England, emitted a jet of water as forceful and as hot as we could wish, though the walls surrounding it had a tendency to leak. As prescribed by government regulations, the laundry was a separate room, leading off the kitchen.

At the front of the house there was a concrete slab or walkway a couple of feet above the ground, on which the children would often play though it became very hot in summer. To the side was a gravelled courtyard shielded from the road by a free-standing white wall and covered by what was described as a 'pergola'. Beyond it was a brick structure serving mainly as a carport, but promising development for other purposes. The house roof was gabled, but with a very shallow pitch of about three degrees, which continued at the same angle down through the pergola and the roof of the carport. The ceilings were similarly angled, immediately under the roof, which was made of 'Stramit' metal sheeting over insulation. The walls of the house were rendered and painted, giving it a simple unpretentious appearance of white walls and stained woodwork. It was small, and very similar to many other houses being built in Canberra and elsewhere in Australia in the late 1960s, but it had a certain simple charm which attracted us to it in the first place.

Another attractive feature was that it had been built on one of the larger blocks of land in Aranda of about a quarter of an acre. This was because it faced onto the outside of a sharp bend in the road and the houses on each side were angled away from it so the boundaries were splayed out, giving us more land than most of our neighbours. It was also more or less flat, whereas the land to the left of us facing from the road sloped steeply upwards. Indeed, as we were to find to our cost, it was not only flat but extremely low-lying.

Although the block was big, it was an unattractive mess of shale, bits of rock and appallingly infertile soil when we moved in. There was not one plant, tree nor any sort of greenery. This had been dry sclerophyll forest, which meant poor soil, but in addition to that it was, as we discovered, what in Canberra parlance was known as a 'fill block'. In matters relating to planning and development, Canberra had a language all of its own, some of it not even recognised in other parts of Australia. Thus the grass verge on the side of a suburban street was known as a 'nature strip', the central reservation in a divided road was a 'median strip', an unplanned path defined by the feet of people walking by the shortest route from point A to point B was a 'desire lane'. This planners' language excited some ribald comment, but was widely used nevertheless.

What was entailed by a 'fill block', in our case at least, was that when the area was opened up for development, it was found that the run-off of water down the long, gentle slope behind where our house was eventually built, created an occasional watercourse alongside what became our block. In order to lift the block above the level of the watercourse many tons of shale and inferior soil were dumped on it and on a number of our neighbours' blocks. This would not have been a terribly serious problem (though the builder had to put in extra-deep piles to ensure the house did not sink), except for the fact that the drains put in to cope with surplus water were laughably inadequate.

We were aware that the area was subject to flooding from shortly after we moved in. Our neighbours told us that water had cascaded past the house after several storms before we arrived. Then one afternoon in January 1970 a freak storm deposited over an inch of rain in less than an hour on Aranda, hail was piled feet deep in our courtyard, and a raging torrent swept through our property and several others in its path, causing a great deal of damage. It was an inch or so short of flooding our house, but went straight through several others. The drains were overwhelmed and their manhole covers were forced off by water spouting into the air from the pressure within.

This became a public issue in Canberra and the local residents formed a pressure group to lobby the Commonwealth Government (which was then directly in control of Canberra affairs) to improve the drainage. We were given bland bureaucratic statements that the drainage had been designed according to engineering standards, to cope with everything up to a 'hundred year flood'. Since the drains had already failed to cope several times within about two years, this was patently ridiculous, but we had a hard fight on our hands against a government and public service unwilling to admit its mistake or spend money to put it right. It was not until about a year later, when a flood in another part of Canberra resulted in some fatalities, that the authorities relented and installed enormously improved drainage.

Despite these traumas we settled in to our house, taking advantage of a government allocation of trees and shrubs to establish a garden, which we tried to make as Australian as possible. Australian trees mostly grow very fast, so it was not long before our peppermint gum, banksias, cinereas, bottle brushes, sharp-needled grevilleas and shallow-rooted cootamundra wattles had reached a considerable size and were able to produce precious shade in the hot, dry summers. We were not so purist as to exclude European trees altogether, and planted a claret ash, a Chinese elm and two or three silver birches, though as these grew much more slowly the Australian appearance of the garden was dominant. Less wisely we planted some bamboos, which proved hard to control in later years.

The house grew as well; the carport structure was soon converted into two small and primitive rooms, one a pottery workshop for Audrey and the other a study for me. Audrey bought a small kiln which was put in the place where the car should have stood. In our household, garage space has always been much too valuable to waste on housing a car. That utilitarian machine has always had to contend with the elements without the benefit of shelter (a problem, however, more acute in England than in Australia because of differences in climate).

We acquired two black cats, one called 'Big' and the other 'Little'. Little eventually grew to be bigger than Big, but the names stuck. Much later, Little found his tail caught in a door which slammed shut in a high wind. The damaged tail had to be surgically shortened by the vet, after which he had an unbalanced appearance.

The girls, Kate and Jane, were settled into the local primary school, which was at the end of our road, and had an aboriginal motto in the Aranda language (Aranda being the name of our suburb). Rupert joined them there in 1972. The school had opened its doors in 1969, and with such a young local population, there was a good community spirit, centred in part on the school. Like most of the buildings in the area, the school buildings were low-rise and blended in well with the landscape.

Kate, in addition to schoolwork, was learning the clarinet, and Jane the violin. Some variety of sporting activities was available for the children as they grew older, including 'Little Athletics', soccer, hockey and of course cricket, organised in a network throughout the suburbs of Canberra. There was so much space in Canberra that sports facilities could be generous. Behind the Aranda Primary School was a multi-purpose sports field which seemed to stretch far into the distance, a broad strip of well kept grass between wooded hills on one side and low rise housing in semi-woodland on the other. The children naturally treated this as their playground.

It was not long before we needed to think about extending the house, which was cramped to say the least for a family with four growing children. Money, however, was limited, and so Audrey, who had long been interested in building techniques, began to explore the possibilities of contracting out the various stages of the building herself. She commissioned a plan for the extra room from the builder who had originally put up the house, and armed with this, went to see the appropriate authorities in order to obtain a 'permit to erect a building'.

In a memorable interview, she was first asked the question: 'why don't you send your husband to see us?'. To this she replied with spirit: 'He doesn't know anything about building'. The interviewer then began quizzing her about what she knew about building techniques, concluding with the question: 'what are you going to do about the soffitting?'. Answering this and other technical questions to his satisfaction, she walked out of his office in triumph - to the amazement of the office staff - as the first woman in Canberra to have been granted the coveted 'permit to erect a building'. The extra room was duly constructed in 1972 and is still standing.

It was in such an environment of Australian spaciousness that Tim spent his early years. His character and determination quickly began to emerge, and at 13 months he suddenly walked. A few days later we went on a family walk in the Molonglo Gorge near Canberra, alongside the Molonglo River, taking a rocky, steep, uneven track for a mile and a half. Tim insisted on walking every step himself, vociferously refusing to be carried. When he began to talk, at about 18 or 20 months, it was in short sentences rather than single words.

The only time he really worried us was when at about 18 months he developed a high fever which led to a convulsion. We made an emergency call to the doctor in the evening, who told us to cool him down and prescribed pheno-barbitone and antibiotics. Tim never suffered a repeat of this episode, and was basically a very healthy child, although he caught pneumonia when he was about seven. On that occasion the doctor threatened to clap him into hospital if he saw him playing on the road again instead of recovering sensibly in bed.

From the age of three he went twice a week to a pre-school (kindergarten), of which there was generous provision in Canberra. Already he had formed particular friendships with two boys his own age which would last for the rest of his life. One was with Rob, a friendly outgoing boy who lived a few houses down our road towards the school, and the other was with Stephen, who lived up the hill behind us. We had put a gate in the fence between the two gardens so that the children could come and go as they pleased. Stephen was a much quieter and more introspective boy, who later turned out to possess remarkable artistic gifts.

The fathers of both of them were, like myself, academics working at the Australian National University (ANU), and both their mothers were schoolteachers. A small group of mothers, including Audrey and Stephen's mother (another Audrey) ran a play group for Stephen, Tim, Rob and two or three other children, where they painted, collected insects, traced leaves, made things with clay, sewed, cooked, made music and gardened, with great energy and enthusiasm.

The early 1970s were times of excitement and change in Australia. Rightly or wrongly, there was a feeling that the country had been led for too long in an unimaginative way, that Australian involvement in the Vietnam war had been a mistake, that economic prospects were excellent and that Australia ought now to assert her own identity as a nation having close links with Asia rather than hold onto the coattails of Britain or the United States. The election of the Whitlam Labour Government in December 1972 after 23 years of uninterrupted conservative rule in Canberra, seemed an event full of hope.

Canberra, as the seat of the Commonwealth (that is, federal) Government, was an intensely political town, and this atmosphere of opportunity bordering upon elation was tangible in 1972 and 1973. A sense of optimism was also emerging (though it was not universally shared) over relations with Japan, the country I was principally engaged in studying. Burgeoning trade between Japan and Australia throughout the 1960s was tending to overlay, if not heal, old antagonisms, and the idea that the two countries could do things together was emerging in the early 1970s. It was all part of a new sense of Australian self-confidence, indeed nationalism of a relatively enlightened kind.

When we went on leave to Britain and Japan at the beginning of July 1973, hope and euphoria were still the prevailing mood; when we returned one year and one international oil crisis later, the mood had turned to one of sobriety, anxiety and even gloom. For a while, however, we were away from the Australian scene and able to experience the northern hemisphere once again.

3 Interlude in Britain

Tim was four and a half years old when we flew to Britain for the first half of my sabbatical leave at the beginning of July 1973. How much he later remembered of our stay in the northern hemisphere I am not sure, but for the family as a whole it was a memorable year. The first half, up to January 1974, was spent at St Antony's College, Oxford, where my main work was to finish a book on Japanese politics, followed by six months in Japan for further research. In retrospect, the task of taking four small children around the world, settling them into schools in two different countries, arranging housing and fixing up the hundred and one things necessary for everyday life in an environment different from the one we had become used to, was sufficiently daunting to make me wonder, 16 years later, at our audacity and optimism. Still, we came through, without major upset, having had many interesting experiences.

The first leg of the journey provided two experiences of a kind we should have preferred to do without. Since air tickets for six people Canberra-Sydney-London-Tokyo-Sydney-Canberra made a gaping hole in the family pocket, we were anxious to save as far as possible on fares. Now our eldest, Kate, was still 11 when we departed from Australia, but by the time we left Oxford for Tokyo she would be 12 and therefore liable for a full fare on the London-Tokyo-Sydney-Canberra legs. Our travel agent, with the ingenuity that some travel agents are able to muster, advised us that we could avoid paying a full fare for Kate by making use of the following stratagem: buy in Australia a single fare to a European airport other than London; stay a few days and buy a ticket from there to London, and beyond (on the open ticket principle) to Tokyo, Sydney and Canberra. Since Kate would have started using her ticket before her twelfth birthday, the whole ticket back to Australia would be valid at half fare.

We chose Amsterdam as the European airport which would both fulfil the need to reduce Kate's fare and provide an interesting place for a few days' holiday before settling in Oxford. We arranged with Audrey's parents that they would come over from England to spend a holiday with us. Unfortunately, in those days before plastic money, the only way in which we could pay for the tickets in Holland was to open an account in a Dutch bank in Amsterdam with a cheque sent from Canberra in good time to clear before our departure. We checked carefully with the travel agent what the fare to be paid in Holland was likely to amount to. He made detailed calculations and gave us a figure, which, with some to spare we duly sent to the main Amsterdam branch of the Algemene Bank Nederlands.

The day after our arrival at a hotel on the Prinsengracht in central Amsterdam I presented myself at the said bank armed with a copy of the bank draft recently sent from Canberra. Thus began a period of waiting, and waiting and waiting. Eventually a puzzled but not unduly solicitous clerk came back and told me she had been unable to locate any record of the transaction. I pressed my case. She went away again and after a further interminable period returned to announce that the account had at last been located. It had been opened in the name of 'James Arthur Ainscow' (Ainscow being my mother's unmarried name and thus my third personal name), in the belief that 'Stockwin' was the place I came from. This, however, was not the end of the story. The task of converting an account which had been opened in one name to another name posed well-nigh insuperable difficulties. It was achieved in the end, but only after a further long period of waiting. I had spent a whole morning in this tedious bank. Not in the best of moods, I withdrew the money in large-denomination guilder notes, closed the account which had just been opened in my real name, and retained for life a deep disillusionment with the whole Dutch banking system.

Even this was not the end of the story, because it turned out when we went to buy the tickets that our travel agent in Canberra had undercalculated the amount of money we should need to pay the return fares. Somehow we scraped together the extra money necessary and were able to buy the tickets. Some money was saved but at considerable cost in time and frayed tempers.

The second unfortunate experience was my own fault. We were travelling with a mountain of luggage as befits a family of six going away for a year. At Sydney airport I picked up a case identical to one of ours which, when it was offloaded at Amsterdam was found to belong to a woman en route for the Bahamas. I had to take it to the Qantas office in Amsterdam where a young Australian official had long telephone conversations in impressively fluent Dutch to find out what could be done about retrieving my case and sending the other one on to the Bahamas. A week or so later I travelled by bus from Oxford to Heathrow Airport and was shown a huge concourse full of errant luggage of all shapes and sizes. I was simply told to look for our case, and within about half an hour, I found it.

Despite these setbacks, Amsterdam was a delight. The weather was extremely hot, like Rome in July or Sydney in January. To us it seemed a Mediterranean city, though Dutch friends have assured us it is rarely thus. The children later remembered the street cafés, a boat trip on the canals and harbour, an expedition to Marken and Vollendam on the Ijsselmeer - traditional though touristy villages with their windmills - and perhaps especially, Rembrandt's 'Night Watch' in the Rijksmuseum. None of the children had ever seen paintings by Magritte before, so that when we took them to a Magritte exhibition, their eyes of experience were opened wide by the sight of trains emerging from fireplaces and portraits of apples suspended in front of men's faces.

They also had a chance to get to know their maternal grandparents, whom they had not seen for some years. One episode which I did not experience remains in the family memory. While I was wasting a morning negotiating at the bank, the rest of the family visited places of interest, and eventually ordered a snack at a café within the Rijksmuseum. Tim's grandmother, Marion (known to the children as 'Grandmarion') ordered him a 'raspberry ripple' ice cream. When this delicacy arrived, Tim announced in a voice which did not invite dissent, that he would not eat it 'if you don't take the red bits out'. Grandmarion thereupon began to dissect

Story of Tim

the ice cream with meticulous care, removing all the red ripples that alternated with the white ripples.

His grandfather Eric ('Granderic') recalls that he had rarely seen anything more remarkable than Grandmarion's attempt, which was successful, unbelievably, to disentangle the pink ripple from the white ice cream with a spoon. But all the time - and it took several minutes - Tim was bawling at the top of his voice, while the whole restaurant of Dutch lunchers looked at them sternly and with total disapproval. They felt like characters from H.M. Bateman. Only when he was satisfied that only white was left did Tim consent to eat the ice cream.

We settled in Oxford, renting a house in Walton Street, near the centre of the city, which had belonged to the late Enid Starkie, a famously eccentric don who used to walk about in a flowing cloak. At the time the area was badly run down, and in the lane behind the house there seemed to be a constant trade, run by teenagers, in stolen bicycles and parts of bicycles. One day I saw a youth being arrested by the police, presumably for drug possession. While we were there the derelict houses across the street were being demolished to make way for the new central university offices and a block of flats for graduate students which threw up a fine dust which settled everywhere.

Nevertheless, it was an interesting place to live, we had a car and the loan of a bicycle, and I could settle down and finish my book. At St Antony's College I was sponsored by a well known scholar, Richard Storry, who wrote lucid and elegant histories of modern Japan. For much of the time I stayed at home and wrote, free of any responsibility except having to give a seminar or two.

Once the new school year started, the children were placed in schools in Oxford. The two girls went to Bishop Kirk School (a 'middle school' in the Oxford system) and Rupert to St Philip and St James' First School (known as 'Phil and Jim'), near St Antony's. It would have been unthinkable that Tim, who still had a few months to go to his fifth birthday, and who was used to pre-school in Canberra, should not go to school as well. Unlike Canberra, however, no places were available in the state sector so at some cost to parental pocket and conscience he went to an independent school called Greycotes, an experience which he greatly enjoyed, including the study of such matters as 'electricily' (*sic*).

There he had a particularly vivacious Canadian woman teacher, who wrote on his end of term report that he was a 'charming boy with a magnetic personality, he is well liked by his classmates, and he, in turn, is generous and kind towards them. [He] has an excellent memory: he stores a tremendous amount of information. His language is well developed and precise. He has begun to read and is justifiably proud of this achievement... A creative child, Timothy is never bored. There is always a problem to solve, a game to play, a new way to handle paint. His enthusiasm inspires others to experiment with him. [He] thoroughly enjoys and exploits dramatic situations in "Music and Movement" and enters into physical activities with enthusiasm...' She also told us she thought he was a 'lateral thinker'.

Tim's maternal grandfather, Granderic, being of a rather sceptical disposition over evidence of intellectual ability in small children, said he found it difficult to take this report seriously. Indeed, a degree of scepticism was probably in order: five-year-old children have a very long way to go before one can really be sure about the extent of their abilities. Nevertheless, there were phrases here which resonated with the reality of Tim in later years: his capacity to enthuse and inspire loyalty in his friends, his ability to concentrate and the scope of his memory for information (he became, for instance, a walking encyclopaedia of cricket, not just the boring statistics but also the evaluation of strategy and form), his creativity, energy, enthusiasm for physical activities, desire to take on new things.

In his teenage years, he did not always find learning easy: languages did not come to him with the facility he would have liked, he was foxed by chemistry (or thought he was), and frequently complained to me that he could not read books at the speed he needed to read them in order to complete his work in time and to read widely. Sometimes his worries about this were quite vociferously externalised within the four walls of our house, and I think on occasion at school. But in the end his determination and ability to concentrate usually won through. This, however, is to anticipate a much later part of the story. There are still a few stories from the second half of

Story of Tim

1973 to relate.

One of Tim's friends from Greycotes was a boy called Avon, who came from an aristocratic family and whose name was prefaced by 'The Hon.' He and Tim shared the characteristic of strikingly blonde hair, and they looked not unlike each other. One Sunday Tim was invited by his nanny to visit him on the family estate outside Oxford and we were all given afternoon tea by her, never meeting his parents. He was several years younger than any of his brothers and sisters, and it seemed that he lived a lonely existence in a house in the middle of a huge park, seeing rather little of his parents. We wondered what the future would bring for him. Tim and he got on well together, but their life chances would assuredly diverge; we never did discover what happened to Avon.

One weekend when summer was long gone and the damp cold of an Oxford winter had already set in, we were visited by Ernest and Mollie, two old friends of Audrey's parents, from London. Ernest's father, in the days when motor cars were infrequent, had been an ostler at the Randolph Hotel in Oxford, and the family had lived in Jericho, a low-lying area of terrace housing near the River Isis (the Thames in its upper reaches), and its large flood plain, Port Meadow, where horses are still left to graze. Much of Jericho has now been gentrified or set up as student lodgings, but in the 1920s it lacked any kind of pretension. We decided to take a walk through Jericho and Port Meadow, partly so that Ernest could show us the area where he had grown up. All the children came with us and after a brisk walk in the cold conditions, we returned by way of a play area with swings and a climbing frame in a street behind the Clarendon Press. Tim immediately perked up and demanded time for 'creative play'. He threw himself into activities, tried to order everyone else around in games of his own devising, to such an extent that Ernest, himself a civil servant, designated Tim as 'obvious administrative potential'. When Tim's interest in the play area showed no sign of flagging, but the rest of us were becoming bored and cold, Audrey and I told Tim it was time to go home to put the dinner on. Immediately he looked around, sized up the situation from the top of the slippery slides, and said: 'you go home and put the dinner on and THESE PEOPLE [Mollie and Ernest] can look after me'.

Sometime before this, in September, we took a trip in the car up north, stayed with my oldest friend from school, John, and his family, who lived in Leeds but were on holiday at a farm east of York. We went on to stay with Audrey's cousin Mick and his wife Wendy and three children, at Greenhead, close to Hadrian's wall. They had lived in Zambia for about ten years, and we had much in common with them as temporary or permanent expatriates. Now they lived in a rambling old farmhouse, with a barn and animals (particularly goats), which was ideal for a gaggle of children. Despite the raw weather (we had not fully acclimatised ourselves to it after Australia), we visited the spectacular Roman fort of Vindolanda nearby, which had only recently been excavated, and where writing on wood had been preserved in unusual soil conditions.

After leaving Greenhead we took Audrey to Carlisle, where she caught a train to Edinburgh for a crafts conference. Such opportunities to be away from the children for a few days were still rare. Meanwhile, the rest of us drove a few miles into Scotland and visited a real Scottish castle, the Hermitage, romantically stark in wild moorland. In its wildness, the area was not entirely unlike some country near Canberra, but to find in such country a ruined castle with turrets and battlements was a new experience for our antipodean children.

From southern Scotland we returned to England and headed for the Lake District, where we stopped overnight at a friendly guest house at the village of Buttermere, next to what is surely the most perfect of all the Lakes. As the four children and I ate a hearty meal at the guest house, the children talked loudly in their strong Australian accents, and I was worried that they might disturb the other guests, who were middle-aged or older. But I found that the north country couple at the next table were intrigued by this unruly family of young Australians, and after we had told them a little about ourselves the husband said with a smile in broad northern tones: 'they're certainly good at talking'.

The next day we parked the car somewhere near the south-eastern end of the Buttermere lake, and walked to the top of Haystacks, which faces the lake from the south. It was hardly an ambitious climb in Lake District terms, but it was a real mountain and the children, including Tim, reached the top without faltering.

The next day we drove back down to Oxford, arriving well after dark, and found to our surprise that our normal route home was blocked by the St Giles' Fair, which was occupying the whole of Oxford's widest street. After a hasty meal, we all trooped out to savour the delights of the fair. The children wanted to go on every ride and try out every stall. But I was tired after driving all the way from the Lake District and eventually managed to drag them home. The only upset of the evening was on the way back to Walton Street, when Tim inadvertently let go of the helium balloon he was carrying and it floated off into the night sky.

Our task during this trip had been to find somewhere to stay in the Lake District for a few days in October when we planned to come up with my parents, who lived in Birmingham. After knocking on various doors, we found Lower Rogerscale Farm, on a remote hillside not far from the town of Cockermouth, whose owners agreed to take us. And so in October we enjoyed a short break in the crisp air and mists and autumn colours of that loveliest part of the north of England (or so I believe; Audrey would disagree and cite the North Yorkshire moors near which she lived for part of her childhood).

My mother had developed a mild heart condition, and could not really climb hills, but we got her up as far as Scale Force, above Crummock Water, where white water crashing down a steep gully created a drenching spray we could hardly escape. On this walk my mother told me a sad story of how a silly quarrel nearly 40 years before, with one of her best friends, who lived in the Lake District, had led to total estrangement between them. She bitterly regretted the quarrel, but it was now too late to make amends for what had happened 'half a lifetime ago'. Hardly aware that there could be such sadness in life, the children, Tim included, climbed the springy turf of those hills with us like mountain goats.

Towards the end of our stay in Britain the international situation started to take on a new instability. First the Yom Kippur war, then the OPEC oil embargo, followed by a fourfold increase in the price of oil on world markets interacting with inflationary pressures already making themselves felt in several countries, created a need for massive and painful economic readjustment. In Britain this manifested itself in industrial unrest and particularly the miners' strike which led to the 'three-day week' and ultimately the fall of the Heath Government. I have a graphic memory of Blackwell's bookshop in Oxford keeping going for the Christmas book trade only by means of a huge generator parked outside on Broad Street.

Just before we were leaving we were faced ourselves with a difficult problem: how to sell the large capacity Vauxhall we had bought second hand a mere six months before. Having received no response whatsoever from an advertisement in the local paper, in one frantic morning I took it successively to ten garages, only to be told at each: 'we are not buying cars for cash' - a negation which applied especially to those which used too much petrol. At the tenth garage, up on Cumnor Hill, I met the same reaction, but I detected the slightest of hints that if I dropped the price far enough they might take it off me. In desperation I more or less said I would sell it to them at any price, and so I was able to get rid of it at just half of the quite fair price I had paid for it six months before. I felt like the victim of an unpredicted stockmarket crash.

Let us let Tim have the last word on this episode in our lives. Just ten years later, in December 1984, when we had been back in England nearly three years and Tim was at school in Woodstock, outside Oxford, he wrote an essay for English on how he felt 'returning to a place that you left some time ago'. The first thing he remembered was the 'stunning red door' on the house we rented in Walton Street. He also recalled 'feeding the ducks in Worcester College at the end of Walton Street. The trees were beautiful and the pond was large and had many ducks. We used to throw small bits of bread into the pond and the ducks would scramble for the food... I really enjoyed feeding them, especially for the first time when I was almost frightened of the birds. It wasn't until last summer that I actually went back into Worcester College grounds and that was to play cricket and not feed the ducks. Nothing seemed to have changed except when I was five I could only remember the duck pond and nothing else about the grounds. Now I think of it, I did remember one other thing. That was a sign on the beautiful mowed grass which said "Keep off the grass".

At the time this bewildered me and I couldn't understand why grass wasn't to be run around on and played on!'

All he could remember about Greycotes school was that he refused to drink the free milk and 'gave it to other people'. But he remembered his brother's school because of an episode which - perhaps fortunately - was expunged from my memory, except for the dimmest shadow of it: 'My brother went to "Phil and Jim" and one thing that I remember vividly about that was when my dad had a mass argument with a parking inspector. My dad and I drove up to the school to pick up my brother and we were a little bit early. There was no where [sic] to park so we parked in front of the school gate. A lady parking inspector came over and insisted us to move [sic] or she would give us a ticket. My dad refused and they both raised their voices in a mass argument. My dad actually swore at her and I had never heard him swear before. How innocent I was! Luckily my brother jumped in the car and my dad drove off and the argument had ended.' Strange that I should have forgotten a 'mass argument'!

It was Tim's memory that was faulty over the Siamese cat called 'Sophie' that we looked after in the house in Walton Street. He wrote: 'She had a beautiful grey coat and one day had four kittens. This came as a shock to us and we knew very little about caring for little kittens. The thing I remembered most was the names we gave the cats. One was called "Choc Cat" because of its dark brown coat, one was called "Brown Bear" because it was the largest and was also brown, and one was called "Little Chicken itsa". This was so called because it was thin and one of my sisters said when first seeing him "It's a little chicken". Also Chickenitsa [sic; actually Chichén Itza] is the name of a town in Mexico! The other kitten's name I can't remember and my parents can't remember it either.'

In fact these kittens were born before we arrived in Oxford and were being looked after by some Americans, who had given them their names. We, however, looked after them for a week or two while the Americans were on holiday and the kittens were already several weeks old. Later on in our stay poor Sophie went on to conceive another litter of no less than eight kittens, but they died inside her and the vet had to remove them by caesarian section.

4 Interlude in Japan

We travelled to Japan, early in January 1974, via Moscow where we changed planes before flying on to Tokyo. It was a long and tedious flight, followed by a slow and uninspiring car journey from the airport in Tokyo to the house a friend had found for us at Hayama on the coast. Between London and Moscow we had one experience that remained with us: low down on the horizon and pink in the sunset was the comet - Kohoutek's comet - that we had been reading about in the newspapers, always with the warning that it was too faint to see with the naked eye. No announcement was made about it on the plane, but there it floated, silent and motionless and hardly noticeable in the fading light, but, when found, so obviously a comet. It was as though we as a family had made the discovery of a beautiful object, the existence of which nobody else suspected.

The three older children had been to Japan before, but so long ago that they remembered little about it. It was Tim's first visit. Our arrival was inauspicious. First of all, everybody was desperately tired; but in addition, the car ride to Hayama (accompanied by our friend, Mieko, who had so generously found us the house) took us through the endless depressing industrial suburbs of the southern part of Tokyo and the towns and cities of Kanagawa Prefecture which stretched south in an uninterrupted sprawl. Japan had been through a long and explosive period of industrial growth, with little regard for the environment, (though policy had already started to change), and Kate, as we went past the umpteenth factory, moaned: 'how much more is there of this industrial stuff?'

When we reached the house in Hayama, we were met by my old mentor, Professor Hayashi and his wife, and by the landlady, who was about to move to Tokyo to stay with her daughter while we rented her house. She was 75 years old and spoke an archaic form of Japanese. She immediately set about explaining to me the workings of various domestic appliances, which I had to translate into English for Audrey, and make intelligent responses, all in a state of extreme fatigue. I remember that neither the words nor the understanding would properly come.

After this was over, Professor and Mrs Hayashi took us for a delicious Japanese meal at the Hikagejaya restaurant in Hayama (famous as the restaurant where the anarchist Osugi Sakae had been stabbed by his girlfriend in 1923). We tried to make conversation as best we could. Noticing that the children were unusually silent, I looked up and saw Jane sitting bolt upright in her chair, fast asleep. When we finally returned to the house, everybody departed and we could spread out the *futon* and go to sleep, we heard, as though in the far distance, the telephone repeatedly ringing. But this did not translate into action to answer it, not as a result of a conscious decision but because our bodies and brains were already anaesthetised against the possibility of any action whatever.

The house in Hayama was a left-over from an earlier age. The design was completely traditional, the construction almost entirely of wood and the floors of every room covered with *tatami* - finely woven straw matting. The house was on two storeys, was large by Japanese standards, and the rooms were separated from each other by sliding paper screens or *shōji*.

Japanese houses tend to be designed with summer heat, rather than freezing winter, in mind, and the outer walls afforded little protection against the cold. All we had as artificial heating was a couple of kerosene stoves, which had to be used carefully as in such a building they were an acute fire hazard, and an electric *kotatsu*, which was a square hole in the floor of the smaller living room, with a low table frame over it, leaving enough room for several people to sit round with their feet and legs in the hole. An electric heater was attached under the table frame, over which was placed a quilt which covered people's legs, and the whole structure was then covered with a detachable table top on which food, or the children's homework, could be arranged. Winters in Japan can be extremely cold, and the *kotatsu* was an oasis of warmth and family togetherness even though we could see our breath at the same time.

Having left Britain in the middle of the 'three-day week', we arrived in a Japan seriously disrupted by the impact of the oil crisis. For a period of a few months before it was brought under control, inflation reached levels unknown for many years. Apparently because of widespread hoarding and speculation, certain goods disappeared from the shops, detergents and toilet paper being the most conspicuous examples. When we went in search of detergent to a general store in Hayama, which was across the Miura Peninsula from the American military base at Yokosuka, we were told by the woman behind the counter that we would have to look for detergents at the PX (special stores for US forces personnel). We explained that we had absolutely nothing to do with the PX, and were not even American, but she still could not help me. Eventually we obtained enough from friends to be able to wash our clothes, and soon the situation eased. But it was a graphic experience of the crisis, which, though quickly overcome, caused a great deal of anxiety at the time.

Professor Hayashi had generously tried to find places for our three school-age children at a local state school, but the school did not feel it could cope with children who spoke hardly any Japanese. He had been more successful, however, when he approached the Principal of the Seisen (Sacred Spring) Primary School in Kamakura, the town near where he lived, and, after some negotiation which we conducted with the Principal ourselves, they were accepted.

The school was run by a Spanish Catholic order of nuns, although virtually all the staff were Japanese (many of them lay teachers), and the Principal herself was a Japanese nun, Sister Yamaji, a formidable personality. She ran the school with a firm hand and attributed many of the problems afflicting Japan to the influence of Communists. The childrens' first experience of the school was daunting: they were taken up onto the stage by the Principal and introduced to the school of six or seven hundred children in a language of which they did not yet understand anything. The girls, with their red hair, felt highly conspicuous in any case, but this initial public exposure was almost too much.

After a week or two, however, they found everybody so friendly that they began to enjoy themselves. Kate and Jane were put into the same class, where they were helped by a girl who had an American father and knew both languages. Rupert, as a seven year-old, was placed in an elementary class with an excellent male teacher. He was much amused to find that counting in Japanese starts with the numbers 'itchy knee', and became expert at *jan-ken-pon* ('scissors, stone, paper'), which he played with his friends on the bus, without the need for language.

Like most Japanese schools, Seisen emphasised mutual responsibility within a class and hierarchy between classes. We went to a school concert where each class put on a performance for the class above it, and two days later a speech day, the formality of which was astonishing. The father of a French girl, the only other foreigner at the school, told us he was sure you could not now find such a formal ceremony at a school anywhere in Europe, except possibly in Germany. But our children's experience was that within a class there was a relaxed and easy familiarity and cheerfulness.

Our strong impression was that the Japanese cultural influences on the school were more pervasive than the influence of Catholic doctrine or practice, though to some extent they may have reinforced each other. At the speech day the Chairman of the Board of Governors made an astonishing speech in which he said that Christianity was the basis of understanding Western culture, and with Japan more and more involved with the Western world, exposure to Christianity during schooldays would help the pupils in later life to understand how to deal with Europeans and Americans. We wondered how much of such influence really percolated through to them in practice. Tim accompanied us on this occasion, and became agitated on concluding, wrongly, that everyone on the platform would have to make a speech.

Another aspect of school was the daily travel there and back. Kamakura was two towns away from Hayama along the coast, and the time it took to travel meant a long day. At around 7.30 in the morning we put the children on a bus outside our house, which went along the slow coast road through Hayama to Zushi, from where they caught a train for one stop to Kamakura, and then a school bus to the school. Since Kate and Jane took Japanese lessons with a woman in Hayama for two days a week instead of going to school, Rupert, at the age of seven, on those days undertook this journey on his own. What struck us forcefully was that many children of his age were doing the same thing with no idea that it was anything out of the ordinary. The trains in the early morning were full of tiny children in school uniforms, chattering away. Public transport was the normal method of travel, and nobody considered it unsafe, even for the youngest of schoolchildren.

Tim was still too young to join his sisters and brother at Seisen School, but as in Oxford we could not have had him twiddling his thumbs at home, so Audrey, accompanied by our friend Mieko, set out one morning to find a kindergarten that would accept him for the duration of our stay. After being rejected by several, including one that was on top of a mountain, they located the Hayama *Yōchien* (kindergarten), which agreed to accept him.

Hayama is an old fishing village which has spread along the coast and into the hinterland, though its development is constrained by mountains behind. The Hayama *Yōchien* was located some distance away from the main coastal road and the approach to it was through a network of narrow back lanes through the town. The procedure for delivering Tim to his *yōchien* was to take him two stops on the bus from our house to a bus stop called Shinnasé at the beginning of the main part of the town. (Japanese characters have alternative ways of pronouncing them, and Shinnasé was far enough from Tokyo that Tokyo visitors would often misread the characters as 'Manasé'.) Here he would be met by one of the *yōchien* teachers, and a crocodile of tiny children would form, which gradually became longer and longer as children were picked up along the way to the kindergarten.

Shinnasé bus stop was directly opposite a beach where in the spring the local women waded out into the shallows and collected seaweed (now, I believe, called in English 'sea vegetable'), and hung it up in long strips on drying racks. On clear days, which mostly occurred in winter, the snowy conical form of Mount Fuji could be seen clearly across the bay some 50 miles away. Tim became fascinated by this beautiful and mysterious mountain, and started his day in a better mood when he could see it than when he could not. He even cried some days when it was not visible. Again on clear days the volcanic island of Oshima could also be seen on the southern horizon.

At the Hayama *Yōchien* there were four or five American children from families connected with the base, so that to some extent English was used at the school. The result was that Tim probably learned less Japanese than his sisters and brother, but he settled into the routine easily enough. Like all the others at the *yōchien* he wore a light-blue smock, a navy hat, carried a yellow satchel and had a school label with his name on pinned to his front. One day the school went on an outing to Aburatsubo (the name means 'Oil Jar') near the tip of the Miura Peninsula and visited a marine park. Tim's hair at that time and throughout his life was extremely fair, and a group photograph taken on that trip was entitled by us 'the white sheep of the family', which amused his grandparents.

When I told friends in Tokyo that we were living at Hayama, they said 'then you must be living near to the *Goyōtei*' (Emperor's Summer Palace), and it was indeed just down the road from us. The *Goyōtei* was on the beach side of a T-junction where the roads had been conspicuously widened and tidied up, but otherwise there was little evidence that it was an unusual place, and the Emperor was never in residence while we lived in Hayama. Part of the Palace had burned down some years before, which may provide the explanation for the imperial absence (more likely, it was because we were not there in July and August, the 'official' summer season).

Behind our house there was a very steep and densely wooded hill, at the top of which several of our neighbours had placed television masts, connected by several hundreds of metres of wire to their TV sets. The area was so hilly that TV reception was poor, and the workmen who came to fix our aerial told us they assumed we would want to sacrifice the educational channel so that we could get better reception on the other seven.

In the summer the undergrowth became so dense that we no longer felt like fighting our way through it to the top, especially because it became a haven for snakes. Above the hill and our house some large sinister-looking black birds called *tobi* or *tombi* (Siberian black kites) wheeled around continuously. One evening in early summer we came home from an outing and found a badly mauled and very dead large black snake in the garden just by the house. Our first thought was that we were the victims of some kind of xenophobic prank. But on calm reflection we became convinced that the snake was merely the victim of one of the *tobi*, who had killed it only to drop it into our garden.

There was also an abandoned and ruined house in thick woodland on the side of a hill nearby. It appeared that it had never had motor access and we wondered how it had ever come to be built. It was now in a sad and probably dangerous state, and gave us an eerie feeling of sudden abandonment, like the *Marie Celeste*. When I went to look at it again several years later, most of the structure had been destroyed by fire. There were other houses in the area which, though still apparently inhabited, gave an impression of long forgotten grandeur.

From my point of view, the only drawback of living in Hayama was that it was a long way from Tokyo. If I went for the day to the University of Tokyo or one of the main libraries, it meant a full two hours travelling each way. Although this was and is by no means an exceptional commuting distance in the Tokyo area, I found it exhausting and impossible to contemplate on a daily basis. The result was that I tended to concentrate work in Tokyo into about two days a week and collect materials which I could then read at home on the other days.

Our old and draughty house turned out to be a pleasant environment in which to work, especially as the weather became warmer. Our landlady had told us not to attempt to repair the *shōji* paper screens if they became torn, as they inevitably did in a household of children: she would 'get a professional to fix them'. The garden was traditionally kept with lovingly tended shrubs, which a gardener was employed to look after. We were not allowed to touch anything in the garden, though Rupert made friends with the gardener and especially enjoyed helping burn leaves and other garden rubbish. As it happened the gardener was an adherent of the Sōka Gakkai sect of Nichiren Buddhism, and tried hard to persuade us to attend a religious festival that the sect was holding. We pleaded other business and never went.

Story of Tim

One morning at about half past eight, the older children had already gone to school and Audrey, Tim and I were sitting at the *kotatsu* for a late breakfast. The electric light that hung from the ceiling suddenly began to swing and we noticed that despite the absence of wind the trees in the garden were swaying. Soon every joint in the wooden house was creeking and objects were banging and crashing with a tremendous racket. We tensed up but did not attempt to move outside, and after a few seconds the earthquake subsided, though there were aftershocks.

In less than a minute the radio, which we were listening to for the news, was interrupting its broadcast to announce that a serious earthquake had occurred, with its epicentre near the Izu Peninsula, 50 or 60 miles down the coast from us. As later reports came in, we learned that the quake had triggered landslides which had engulfed houses and that there had been a number of deaths. When the children returned from school that evening, they announced that they had been ordered under their desks as soon as the earthquake began happening. Their Japanese friends accepted it as routine.

With the children at school or kindergarten, Audrey was able to renew her experience of Japanese pottery, and took lessons from a woman potter who lived just by the railway station at Kita-Kamakura (North Kamakura), near a lovely temple called Enkakuji. She was a lively and uninhibited lady who gave classes for local housewives and was very partial to whisky. She was also a good potter and teacher of her craft. Audrey also took some lessons from another potter in Kamakura and went on several expeditions out of Tokyo with Mieko to visit pottery areas.

On the most ambitious of these, while I looked after the boys in Hayama, they took Kate and Jane for a week or so on a tour of potteries in several regions, most importantly the Bizen area on the Inland Sea round Okayama, where unglazed pots are fired in the kiln wrapped in straw, which, in burning, deposits ash on the pots and creates a kind of glaze. Because of the uncertainty of this process, there is a 20 per cent failure rate of pots in most kilns, but the successes are hard to surpass.

Years later Mieko told us the following story: one day she was at the house of our New Zealand friends, Geoff and

Aurelia, who lived five minutes walk away, when Tim unexpectedly wandered into the house. Mieko said to him that he looked like his grandfather (Granderic), whom she had met in England. Tim made clear that he did not appreciate this comparison and said: 'I don't like a man who tells me that Coca Cola is poison'. Tim had taken this example of his grandfather's humour far more seriously than was presumably intended.

During the last few weeks that we spent at Hayama, it was warm enough to swim off the beach, and once or twice we went a few hundred metres out to sea with Geoff and Aurelia, who owned a small dinghy. Towards the end of our stay the beach, and the town generally, was being prepared for the summer influx of tourists. The Japanese at that time maintained a rigid definition of the swimming season as July and August only, so that the beach could be nearly deserted up to 30 June, but with barely a square metre free on 1 July. Although we had to return to Australia just before the summer season began, we saw the erection of a long line of temporary wooden stalls, selling *soba* (buckwheat noodle soup), *sushi*, beer and other provisions for tourists. The beach, which was normally something of a rubbish tip, was now going to be swept meticulously every day by workers employed specifically for the purpose.

Our landlady now returned from Tokyo, and stayed in the house to prepare it as a holiday home for the two months of the 'season' for employees of a big company, who would pay her 10 to 20 times the rent we were paying, and would have up to 40 of their people staying in it at one time. How the house could accommodate so many people was difficult for us to imagine, though when we thought about it we could see that in the virtual absence of furniture there was indeed space for 40 or so bodies to sleep side by side on the *tatami*. Privacy, after all, was hardly the most respected value in the average Japanese company; creating a sense of togetherness was deemed much more important.

Our children experienced many things in Japan. Kate and Jane both went to music lessons, Kate with a clarinettist from the Tokyo Philharmonic and Jane with a local violin teacher. We took them to visit many of our Japanese friends. The girls were worried about slipping back in their ability to read English, so in the evenings we would read with them a book borrowed from Professor Hayashi, which was hardly what they would have read at home: a historical and cultural guide to Kamakura (a former capital of Japan), written in a Japanese version of ponderous 1920s English.

When the children were home from school, they liked to watch a programme called *kamen raidā* (Masked Riders) on TV, an animation series about a group of young people with semi-supernatural powers who went through numerous adventures in the service of society. It had polish and style and a deftness of touch that remained in the memory. They liked *sumō* wrestling and *kaijū* (monsters), and Snoopy which was hugely popular among Japanese children. When the time came for us to leave one of their friends brought as a present a large model of Snoopy, weighing several kilograms, which he had made out of clay and papier mâché. Alas, overloaded as we already were, we could not carry it with us, and had to leave it with friends. But we all remembered it as a symbol of Japanese generosity and friendship.

5 Growing up in Australia (I)

When we returned to Canberra from Japan at the beginning of July 1974, Tim was five and a half, and could follow his brother and sisters into the Aranda Primary School, a mere three minutes walk away at the end of the road. He stayed there until the end of 1980, when he graduated to the Canberra High School, located beyond the playing fields, and still within walking distance. It was a stable period, and in a superficial sense an uneventful one, in which he and his cohort of friends learned many things and grew in experience together. Some of what he learned was routine rather than inspired, though doubtless none the less valuable for that: In September 1976 he was writing in a school exercise book such statements as: '6 + 10 = 16; there were sixteen birds altogether'.

More imaginatively if less accurately, at an uncertain date, he wrote an unfinished story which began: 'In a town in England a famous astronoma discovers a planet imbetween Earth and Mars, Professa Xionides (the sinentist) desides to call it after his name.' Later on, the story includes the following piece of dialogue: 'Jenny: But all the planets have been dicovered its imposable. Xionides: This one has been made recently I think because it wasn't there 1 month ago. Jenny: Oh, another thing how will we get there? Xionides: Today I planned a very powerful rocket it will take 6 people each will have their own room and is just like a house which flies. It takes 3 gallons to 6,000 miles, think of it, wouldn't it be nice? Jenny: it would be nice, but it would take years to make and think of all the money it would use up. Another thing how many miles is it away from the Earth? Xionides: I haven't found out yet all I did was look at it and rushed home to tell you. Jenny: I still don't believe you.'

How far this tale of male enthusiasm confronted by female scepticism came from observation of his own family is difficult to say. Certainly from the family's perspective he was becoming its most irrepressible member, and this led to repeated attempts by his elders to shut him up when he insisted on talking all the time. On some things, notably food, he could be unbearably fussy, which led to predictable expressions of irritation from the rest of the family. He would be described as 'a little brat' or worse.

Once, when Grandmarion and Granderic were staying with us at a friend's beach house at Tuross, southeast of Canberra, Tim annoyed Rupert so much that Rupert picked him up, threw him on the floor and stood on him. Curiously enough, being the youngest family member did not mean that he was indulged, but rather he felt that he had to work extra hard to keep up, which was true to a considerable extent. Being smaller and younger than everybody else may have its advantages, but it also has disadvantages if all the rest are vigorously pursuing their own activities and expecting you to stay abreast. When Tim was about eleven, Kate, in reflective mood, commented to me that he was extremely competitive. Perhaps competitiveness was born within him, but it must surely have been drawn out to its full potential by being the baby of an active family.

It was a family, indeed, in which every member was remarkably distinct in personality and interests. Although these revealed themselves only gradually, in retrospect they can be traced back to fairly early childhood. Each of us had a set of interests which on occasion would become a focus for family activity.

With Kate music was an abiding passion. From the age of about seven she began learning the clarinet, and continued, under a succession of teachers, until she became a full time student at the Canberra School of Music after leaving school, and later, a professional orchestral player. Over many years the sound of clarinet practice was a normal feature of evenings at home, and even now to hear certain pieces of music, such as Mozart's clarinet quintet, is to recreate that time. Both Kate and her sister Jane, a violinist, joined the Canberra Youth Orchestra, which rehearsed on Saturday mornings. In 1980 we all joined in an ambitious and at times nightmarish fund-raising effort to send the Orchestra half way round the world to the International Festival of Youth Orchestras in Aberdeen. They also gave concerts in Cologne, Bonn, Paris and at

Waterlooville in Hampshire.

Jane was also interested in music and learned to play the violin well, but without any intention of becoming a professional musician. She loved making things, and at one stage considered the possibility of making musical instruments. Years earlier, when she was five or six and we had recently moved to Aranda, Jane started what she called, for reasons I have forgotten, the 'Spotty Café' for her family, initially with vegemite and peanut butter sandwiches, later with elaborately written menus and elegantly prepared food. This interest was to grow in later years until she became a professional chef making the world's most beautiful and creative wedding cakes.

Rupert pursued a number of interests, including at various times the trumpet, sport (successively soccer, hockey and long distance walking) computers, pop records and much later motor bikes. But what he really consistently enjoyed above all else was the natural world: animals, trees and the Australian bush, which was never far away in Australia's 'bush capital'. Once he went away on a camp in the Riverina area of southern New South Wales, and on his return talked with gleaming eyes about the camp's pet python, called 'Monty' (naturally) which had coiled itself around the arms and necks of him and his friends.

We kept a fluctuating number of large lizards, which were able to wander freely around the house, but often lived under the fridge. Most of these were shinglebacks, which looked like pieces of retread shed on the highway, and blue-tongues with smooth skins, long tails and a darting tongue in metallic blue. Once we had to take one of the cats to the vet, and Rupert came along carrying one of the blue-tongues under his coat. At the appropriate moment he revealed it to the vet and asked why this one should have an indentation in its spine. But the vet said he had only ever been to 'half a lecture' on lizards, and was not able to help except by applying general principles to the problem. Within the family Rupert was famous for the expression 'isn't he gorgeous!', often applied on encountering quite unappealing examples of the local fauna.

For Tim there was also a variety of activities which he pursued at different times, but sport became his passion. For a while he also learned the violin, and attained a certain elementary standard, but peer pressure and perhaps a lack of innate enthusiasm led him to drop it after a certain stage. Later he learned to play the drums and this became a more permanent interest. He became an enthusiast for a pop group called 'Kiss', which created a kind of fantasy world with extravagant body and facial painting. His mind was active, and a friend who visited us at around that time remembers Tim asking, out of the blue, 'How many seconds are there in a year?'.

But sport ruled. From some time after we returned from Japan he belonged to the Belconnen Soccer Club and played in teams appropriate to his age group. The coaching was skilful and enthusiastic as several of the local coaches were originally from Yugoslavia, where soccer is an obsession. Just before I left for a conference in Mexico followed by a trip to the west coast of the US in August of 1976, I watched his team win a difficult victory against strong opposition. This put them in contention for the championship, but I did not learn that they had actually won the championship until I returned home about three weeks later. His team also ended up 'Premiers' four years in succession from 1978 to 1981.

In 1976 and 1977 he regularly went to 'Little Athletics' with Rupert and collected a number of certificates, but abandoned this activity in favour of cricket, which he had desperately wanted to play earlier but for which he had been too young. Then, every summer he played a great deal of cricket, again in local suburban teams, and gradually developed talents as a batsman and a wicket keeper. Something in the tradition and atmosphere of Australian cricket must have interacted with his personality because long after he had left Australia the cricket he had learned on the pitches of Canberra as a young boy remained his inspiration.

Even when his teens were still well in the future, he was serious about sport and aimed for perfection. Once, aged ten or eleven, when he was kicking a soccer ball, Audrey told him to 'stop playing around with that ball'. 'I'm not playing', replied Tim, 'I'm practising'. Again, after a cricket match, when he was bowled after scoring a good number of runs, she told him it was bad luck that he had been bowled. To this he replied: 'No, I've failed, because I failed to protect the wicket'.

There were other activities too. He was in the cubs for a

while, and became a 'sixer' in 1979, but he never went on to the Scouts. As he always seemed to be so busy, he acquired the nickname 'bumblebee', mainly used by Audrey, and this stuck with him to the end.

In this tour round the family let us not forget the parents, who, even with the children becoming progressively more independent in their activities and ideas, may be thought to have retained some background influence. We were also useful, indeed vitally necessary, as a free taxi service to sports fixtures, music lessons and other appointments. The Volkswagen Kombi van we bought in 1974 (and its similar successor bought three or four years later), clocked up an enormous mileage.

Audrey, once we were settled back in Canberra, quickly moved to put her talents in making stoneware pottery (and some porcelain) onto a really professional basis. With some outside help she built a 15 cu.ft. kiln out of white firebricks. She extended the pottery and rationalised the production. She worked long hours, and her work became sought after locally and to some extent elsewhere.

Every year on the last Sunday in November she held an exhibition and sale of her work in our garden, to which many people came. The children and their friends were mobilised to man each of several trestle tables on which the pottery was displayed. A system of issuing tickets was carefully devised to avoid 'double selling', and I sat, with one of our friends, at the cash box in the courtyard, describing this as 'my one day of the year as a businessman'. These events were held every November between 1974 and 1981, and on each occasion the weather was clear and hot. Apart from pottery and the local Crafts Council, she played the flute a little in a wind group with friends, occasionally attended a book discussion circle, knew many people and was homemaker and unfailing source of advice.

6 Growing up in Australia (II)

In my own life, work naturally occupied the largest part. Teaching in a large university department, there were courses to prepare, students to look after, administrative tasks to perform, political battles to fight. As a specialist on contemporary Japan, I had to read a great deal in order to keep up with what was happening in that complicated country. Both Japan and indeed Australia were going through a painful period of adjustment following the first oil crisis. Midway through 1975 I was asked to spend most of a year attached as 'academic in residence' to the Commonwealth (i.e. federal) Government's Department of Foreign Affairs.

It was while I was there, on 11 November 1975, that Australia's greatest constitutional crisis occurred, with the dismissal of the Whitlam Labour Government by the Governor-General, Sir John Kerr. When the news came through to the office where I was working, the effect was extraordinary. Whereas one or two of the typists and filing clerks appeared not displeased by the news, virtually all the diplomatic staff were in a state of shock which did not dissipate for several days. The atmosphere in Canberra between then and the general election about a month later (which led to the election of a conservative government under Malcolm Fraser), was electric, and it is probably true to say that the political divisions in Australia created at this period did not heal until the 1980s.

The immediate issues that had led to the crisis were complex and there is little agreement on the apportionment of blame, but the feeling that the Governor-General in cutting the Gordian knot was an unelected official dismissing the legitimate elected government of the country ran deep, at least among the people I knew. This was an opinion I strongly shared, and it coloured my view of Australian governments during the latter half of the decade.

Not quite all corners of my life were work, however. About this time I bought a small sailing dinghy of the 'Heron' class, joined the YMCA Sailing Club and raced against others of the same class at weekends. I had sailed as a teenager in England, and taught a little of the art of sailing to the children, though with their many competing interests, none of them ever became enthusiasts. Lake Burley Griffin, the artificial lake with more than 20 miles of coastline which winds through the centre of Canberra, was a pleasant piece of water to sail, though Sydneysiders tended to compare it dismissively with their spectacular Harbour.

Rupert and Tim complained that the boat was too slow and that we never won races, but I was never much attracted to the flashier craft that populated the lake. With local friends from our suburb, who also sailed with the YMCA Sailing Club, we shared frequent picnics, barbecues and other social occasions during our last years in Canberra. Twice we took the boat on a summer holiday to the shores of Lake Jindabyne in the Snowy Mountains, where fierce winds whip up the lake surface from gullies between the mountain slopes, and we could sail for hours without running out of lake.

The family was attached to skiing as a pastime much more than sailing, especially as the ski slopes of the Snowy Mountains were an easy drive from Canberra. After we returned from Japan in 1974, we began an invariable annual routine of renting a caravan for a week in one of the two caravan parks in the tourist town of Jindabyne, on the southern shore of the lake.

The road to Jindabyne from Canberra goes due south through increasingly treeless countryside on the Monaro Plains through the town of Cooma, a pioneering settlement which in the 1950s became the headquarters of the ambitious Snowy Mountains hydro-electric scheme. In the 1970s it was a thriving small town spreading out on either side of a main street which switchbacked, broad and straight, over the dips and hills on which the town was built. Many times we had breakfast at the same Greek restaurant with its long bar and alcoves of hard benches, next to the central park reservation which boasted a modern concrete and steel bandstand and flew the flags of all the countries whose nationals had worked on the Snowy Mountains scheme. Cooma was some 65 miles to the south of

Canberra and Jindabyne about 40 miles further on into the mountains to the south-west. It was always an exciting moment when we came over the hill overlooking Lake Jindabyne and saw across the lake the bare white peaks of the Snowies glistening white above the olive green snow gums of the lower slopes.

Life in the caravan park was far from luxurious and one disastrous winter the rain began shortly after we arrived on a Sunday and never ceased until the following Thursday, converting the caravan park into a muddy mess and ruining any idea of serious skiing. Most times, however, we would set out in the mornings from Jindabyne and drive to one of the nearby resorts, usually Perisher Valley, and spend the day on the slopes. The first time Tim saw snow, when he was very small, somewhere on the road above Jindabyne, he wanted to know 'who painted it on?' By the late 1970s he, like his sisters and brother, was becoming an accomplished and experienced skier, and they easily out-skied their sedate and unskilled parents, who had first come to know each other on a ski-slope in France. Rupert once pulled a ligament in his knee, but they never suffered any broken bones.

Living cheek by jowl alongside everybody's wet ski gear in the caravan occasionally provoked complaints. There was the occasion when Audrey and I went out to a French restaurant in Jindabyne to dine on escargots, leaving the children with bangers and mash. Once also in the caravan I clumsily dropped a saucepanful of spaghetti into a sink of soapy water, then after washing it rather quickly served it up *faute de mieux*. We were not easily allowed to forget these incidents: 'Dad, you remember when you dropped the spaghetti into the sink and then GAVE IT TO US TO EAT!...'

There was also the occasion when the accelerator cable of the van froze in extremely cold conditions at Perisher Valley and we had to negotiate the road out of the valley with an engine that would only run at high revs. When we took it to a garage in Jindabyne, with the whole car smelling of burning clutch material, the mechanic to whom we explained the problem said: 'who ever heard of an accelerator freezing up?' Subsequently no garage was ever able to prevent this unheard-of problem from recurring. Another time when we were leaving the snow, a colony of wombats appeared from their burrows at the side of the road in the snow, and the spectacle of these lumbering reclusive creatures appearing in broad daylight for all to see had everyone stopping their cars to take photographs.

Most summers we would pile our things in the van and drive down the winding mountain road off the Southern Tablelands to the New South Wales south coast. Several times we rented a white wooden house on the cliffs over the beach at Bermagui, which had a tiny harbour where we could buy fish straight off the fishing boats. Once, when we had bought some gemfish and Rupert was preparing them for cooking in the kitchen, he said in his strong Australian accent 'I can't get this bloke's head off', and from then on fish were 'blokes'.

The most ambitious summer trip we did together was to Kangaroo Island in South Australia, a large island off Adelaide which is about the size (and shape) of Cornwall. We set off at about five a.m. on a chilly Canberra morning, aiming to reach Mildura near the New South Wales - South Australia border by nightfall. For much of the journey the road is as unbending as a taut string, as it crosses the flat - unbelievably flat - and almost featureless plain to the north of the Murray River past desolate-looking townships such as Hay and Balranald. Every hour of that long day the temperature rose further, and by the time we had covered the five hundred odd miles to Mildura the wind blowing into the van through its open windows could have come straight from a blast-furnace. At five in the evening we booked into a caravan park at Mildura and found that the outside surface of the caravan we rented burned the skin if we touched it. Several families were sitting outside their caravans watching TV sets they had brought with them, the better to enjoy their annual holidays spent in the searing heat of a Mildura caravan park.

The next night we stayed with friends in Adelaide, and the following morning put the car on the ferry to Kangaroo Island, landing at the little settlement of Kingscote, where most of the island's population of a few thousand people lives. We still had a drive of about 60 miles on gravel roads to a farm near the western end of the island where we were to stay. The nearest shop was 40 miles away at Vivonne Bay on the island's south coast to the east of us. The Mildura caravan park returned to haunt us on the island because Kate, Jane and Rupert had taken a long swim in the park's small and overcrowded swimming pool, thereby picking up a nasty throat infection which appeared a few days later. Tim missed out on this because he was recovering from mumps and was not allowed to swim.

We all, however, piled into the van for a journey to the doctor, who was the wife of a farmer in the centre of the island and practised from home. Their farm, like most of the others that we saw, looked anything but prosperous, and indeed the island as a whole seemed economically depressed. Some of the land was given over to farming, but much of it was undisturbed bush, and every time we went out in the van we were liable to encounter wallabies, kangaroos, possums, echidnas and other wildlife. Indeed animals were more of a driving hazard than other vehicles. The children were able to converse with a colony of seals at Seal Bay on the south coast.

My strangest memory of this hauntingly beautiful island was an image of human isolation. We were shown round a lighthouse at a remote part of the north coast, accessible on a barely driveable track, by the lighthouse keeper, who I think was of Polish origin. Nearby were two adjoining houses, one in which he lived and one for his assistant. They were probably the only houses for 15 or 20 miles. I commented that the two families must see a lot of each other, to which he replied: 'no, there's absolutely no need to socialise with your neighbours'. In the early nineteenth century a few convicts had managed to escape to Kangaroo Island, which at that time was uninhabited, and somehow managed to live off the land, some of them with Aboriginal women they brought from the mainland. Many ships, sailing to Australia from Britain, foundered against the rocks of the island's coastline and the wrecks are still marked on tourist maps. It is difficult to imagine a more lonely place for any human beings who survived.

By the late 1970s we were quite clear that Australia was home. Audrey and I had taken Australian citizenship in 1976, after the rules had been changed so that British passport holders with Australian residence but not citizenship now needed a re-entry visa on returning to Australia from overseas. This change was part of the assertion of Australian nationhood that emerged in the 1970s and was to lead to the ending of special status for those British origin. We ourselves were in general sympathy with this assertion of national identity by our adoptive country, and took Australian citizenship (without, however, losing British citizenship) partly as a matter of convenience and partly as an expression of commitment. It seemed appropriate that Shugo, one of our Japanese friends, was with us as a participant in the naturalisation ceremony, at which the order of ceremony was read by a lady who spoke with the soft lilt of the Scottish Highlands. Our children, of course, had Australian nationality by birth, and British by patriality.

In March 1980 we held a party for our friends to celebrate '20 years of marriage, 20 years in Australia and a new house extension'. It was a memorable occasion, at which most of our friends, as though by collusion, brought us pot plants, many of them large and exotic. These decorated the new living room at the front of the house as part of the new extension which now gave us abundant living space. If the party, however, symbolised that we had all now properly taken root in Australian soil, it was not to last; in less than two years we uprooted ourselves and returned to Britain.

In the late 1970s we were becoming increasingly concerned about the children's grandparents, all of whom remained in Britain. Audrey's parents, Marion and Eric, visited us in the Australian summer of 1977-8, but Marion sadly and unexpectedly died in January 1979. My parents, who were approaching their 80s, were not in good physical shape, and I flew over to see them in Birmingham in 1977, and again in 1979 and 1980, becoming increasingly concerned about their ability to look after themselves. As is often the case with old people, they entirely resisted any attempt to move them into sheltered accommodation or out of the large and draughty house where they had spent the previous four decades and more of their married life. In short visits from Australia I seemed quite powerless to improve the situation.

During my stay in Britain in July 1979 I visited Oxford and found that a new institute of Japanese studies had just been funded. A chair of modern Japanese studies was to be created.

When this was duly advertised early the next year, I decided to put in an application. I remember writing the application one afternoon in my office and sending it off without having much of a sense that this was an action of particular importance, or that I had the slightest chance of success. Before I went to Britain to see my parents in July 1980, I wrote to Oxford to say that I would be available for interview, but they told me they could not get the interview panel together in the vacation, which I interpreted as meaning that my application was not being seriously considered.

When out of the blue in November I received a request to come for interview, flew to Britain in December and was offered the job, we were suddenly faced with an unexpected and perplexing decision. It was a promotion, an opportunity, an adventure, I needed a change of work atmosphere, we would be closer to the grandparents, and so on and so on, but none of us wanted to leave our beloved Australia, the move to new schools might disrupt the children's education, we would be leaving so many friends of long standing, we had heard unfavourable things about life in contemporary Britain, the financial implications were uncertain, and so on and so on.

The timing of the decision that had to made was also difficult: Audrey went into hospital for a gall bladder operation while I was being interviewed in Oxford, and I was due to start a six-month period of research in Japan from January 1981. We considered and argued and weighed the various sides of the case, and went over all the arguments time and time again. In the end I telexed my acceptance, and it was agreed that we should move to Oxford by January 1982. Next day I flew to Tokyo and was there till the end of June. Audrey joined me for two months in the northern spring.

But Tim must have the last word in this chapter. In May 1980, at eleven and a half years old, he went to stay for three weeks in the Philippines with the family of a school friend called Richard, whose father had been posted to Manila on Australian Government business. The family lived in Makati, a wealthy and in part expatriate suburb of Manila. Tim and Richard seem to have spent much of their time playing tennis, but for the first time in his life he saw people living in poverty, and the contrast between extremes of wealth and poverty. The diary he wrote of his stay mentioned this briefly in a factual way (the diary has not survived), and also recorded his extreme anxiety after he accidentally broke Richard's tennis racket, and subsequent relief that it had not spoiled their friendship as he feared at first it might.

In the first half of 1981 Tim wrote a series of letters to Japan, telling me (and Audrey for the two months she was there) about his activities. He had just started at Canberra High School, where the work was harder than he was used to, but also playing several sports, learning the drums and practising BMX riding. While Audrey was in Japan he stayed with the family of his friend Rob, and enthused about the cooking. In a letter dated 11 March he wrote: 'That night we had a beautiful dinner, it was a kind of lamb rolled up in a kind of circle, it was delicious. We had it the next night and it was beautiful again. Tonight we had this beautiful kind of dish thing called "Toad in a hole". Rob's Mum said that you probably have never heard [of] it before.' On 18 March he wrote in the same vein: 'We are having the most beautiful dinners possible and have even better puddings.' On 25 March: 'Rob's Mum buys this beautiful chocolate spread with nuts in it. It is called "Nutella" and I hope we can get some when you come back.'

One day at this time, he was required to bring an apron to school; it was open to him to buy one or to make one. However, he was told by his schoolteacher that if he were really resourceful, he could make one using a sewing machine. With great intensity and deliberation, he sewed tabs onto a teatowel and produced a respectable apron. When it was finished he had put so much effort into it that he was visibly white and drained.

He often included a commentary on world affairs, especially relating to sport. On 4 February he related a famous incident as follows: '...The most strangest thing happened in the third match when on the last ball of the match New Zealand needed 6 to win and Trevor Chappel was the bowler. Greg Chappel really wanted to win this match so he told his brother to bowl an under-arm bowl so New Zealand couldn't hit a six. This was in the rule book and it caused so much fuss that they changed the rules the next day. After the series Greg Chappel surprisingly got man of the series.' Again on 4 March: 'The other thing which is very interesting but I don't know much about is that there is this new brilliant argentinian soccer player that is only 19 years old. A team in Argentina have just bought for 10 million dollars and he is the most expensive soccer player ever. The newspaper people say he is the best player in the world ever and he is alot better than Pelay and Bechanbau. Pelay and Bechanbau were bought for 6 million each before and they used to be the most expensive players. The only thing that I wish I really could do is see this player play. His name is Maradona.' (It took years before I could persuade Tim that 'a lot' was two words, not one.) On 14 May: 'I have just heard that the pope was shot and they have arrested a man. I don't know much about it but I know that he is alright.'

Shortly after Audrey returned from Japan, she took the children to Bermagui, and on 5 May Tim informed me that: 'Last night we had our first fish dinner [which] was called Mowan and it was beautiful. Since Rupe is still in Canberra on a computer coarse and is coming down tomorrow, I had to de-gut the fish and it was great fun. First came out these huge things like sausages then came all the squishy parts and it was hard to get a good grip on the little bits. Anyway Jane cooked it superbly and I loved it.' On 14 June he reported on his schoolwork in the following terms: 'I have just done my homework for the weekend and it was all about angles in maths. As usual noone can help because they say they don't understand. I managed to do all my other and the maths but it took longer than I wanted it to. We have now got a new art teacher... and he is really nice. He always tells the class to go and watch Canberra play who-ever [they're] playing in soccer before the weekend. All my other classes are going well but I don't think I will get an A in any subjects at all at the moment and the next assesment period is in a few weeks. I probably will get Bs and Cs.'

Some five years later, at his school in England, he had to write a poem called 'My Childhood Memories'. The last three verses read thus:

Growing up in Australia (II)

Darambal street tough guys
fights from the cubby house
Then somehow friends again
but soon I was ten

Oh No, frightening Canberra High School
do you really get head flushed down the loo!
Not so bad after all
playing alot more football
A top score of 47 for Wests
we were the best

But best of all were ski holidays
with hot chocolate and powder snow
England, what do you want to go there for?
I don't know.

7 Changing Country

We arrived in Oxford on New Year's Eve 1981. The winter of 1981-1982 was the coldest for many years, and before Christmas the country had experienced heavy snow and low temperatures. At the time we arrived there was a thaw, which was to prove short-lived. To us, though, straight from Canberra midsummer, everything seemed cold and bleak. It was hard to believe that the light was almost gone by the middle of the afternoon. The University had reserved a house near the centre of the city for us to rent temporarily. After two days and nights without sleep we were grateful for a house that was cheerful and warm, with a central heating system that was doing its work with great effectiveness. The house was a superior Victorian terrace, narrow and tall, on five levels with many staircases.

Soon after we moved in, the water stopped running from the taps. Investigation showed that no water was coming into the central heating system from the outside and that this was because a section of the pipe connecting the mains supply with the house had been removed (presumably it had frozen in the cold weather) and had never been replaced. Our good friends Hedley and Mary, who had met us off the plane at Heathrow, brought us to Oxford and settled us in the house, managed to persuade the University maintenance people to send a plumber, whose cheerfulness appeared not unconnected with the fact that it was already well into the evening of 31 December, and who replaced the missing section of pipe. We wondered if the system would have blown up or set fire to the house if the central heating boiler had drained dry.

A few days after we arrived, the winter's second instalment of snow arrived, accompanied by a hideous meteorological phenomenon called 'freezing fog'. The children, for whom snow was strictly reserved for mountain ski resorts, for the first time in their lives experienced an urban snowscape. The ancient and unreliable car we had borrowed from my mother became a lump in a snowdrift outside the house. One day a local tabloid had the banner headline on its front page:

MOSCOW −16°C
OXFORD −20°C

That morning before breakfast Kate washed her red hair and then went out for a run. When she returned her hair had frozen into a solid mass of white crystals. 'That', said an American student at my college who knew about such conditions, 'is a real no-no'. But why should a young Australian be deterred from her morning run by a spot of British frost?

Pipes froze, everything was disrupted and the local press commented unfavourably on Oxford's ability to cope with the snow by comparison with nearby towns such as Reading. But we found that the British, who refused to talk to each other when crossing the Sahara until they had been introduced, suddenly became social and cooperative beings. Cars parked on cambered suburban streets were stuck there unless manhandled into the middle of the road, and any car with spinning wheels was pushed out of its predicament by anyone who happened to be passing. After the snow melted everyone went back to their arm's length behaviour, but it was revealing to see the possibilities beneath the exterior. Now, and for months and even years afterwards we were all looking at Britain with Australian eyes, the children especially, but also Audrey and I, who found that our deepest assumptions about the British way of life were a compound of a contemporary Australian perception with direct experience which was more than twenty years out of date.

Only the boys were still of school age. Kate had finished school in Canberra and had done two of the four years of her course at the Canberra School of Music. It did not seem practicable or desirable to interrupt her course and so she was only with us until the Australian long vacation finished at the end of February. Her boyfriend Chris and two of his friends stayed with us also for a while so that the house was lively with young people. Jane had finished school in Canberra shortly before we left, and in Oxford found a job in a shoe shop for a few weeks before discovering more congenial employment as a silver service waitress in the Randolph Hotel. In October 1982 she went to Westminster College in London, to study catering.

Rupert and Tim entered local comprehensives - Rupert the Cherwell School and Tim the Oxford Boys' School off the Cowley Road. The headmaster of the latter knew Tim had played much cricket in Australia, and as a cricket fanatic was prepared to admit him, even though technically he was too young. Rupert was entering the British system in the middle of the O-level course and had a difficult time of it, finding it hard to adjust at that stage of his education. For Tim, in work terms, it was easier because no exams were in prospect and he could look forward to having nearly all of his secondary education in the same education system.

Tim gradually settled into his school, even though he was a year too young, but he was acutely conscious of being Australian among boys with British loyalties and attitudes. Later he learned to turn his Australian-ness to advantage, but at this stage it was still a shock to discover how different he was. He was still small for his age, and found the school rougher than he was used to. He had not been at a boys-only school before, and he missed the moderating and softening influence of girls. Several times he came home upset that he had been deliberately pushed down the school steps by boys who were older and bigger than himself. There may have been a certain amount of racial friction at the school, which again would have been a new experience for him. The school catchment included working class areas near the Cowley car works along with parts of the city where university families lived, and it was a school which was trying hard to keep academic standards high.

When his Canberra friend Rob had stayed in Oxford some time before with his family, he had joined a football team called the 'Summertown Stars', and Tim was able to join it too, shortly after we arrived in Oxford. In the freezing cold of snowbound January evenings either Audrey or I would take him to 'football practice' (not 'soccer' any more) on a pitch in the suburb of Wolvercote, lit by arc lights. The principal coach was a north-country Oxford geographer who had an almost poetic dedication to the task of training boys in the subtler manoeuvres of the game. When a boy kicked a particularly effective or difficult shot, the coach, who kept up an inimitable banter, would shout 'that's magic!'.

The team played on Saturday afternoons at its home ground off Five Mile Drive in north Oxford or in away matches. It was a talented team which included one or two boys who had ambitions to become professional footballers, and they were league champions in the Oxford Boys' League for 1981-2, and cup winners for 1982-3.

Tim found that he was not quite as good, relative to the rest of the team, nor as well regarded as he had been in Canberra. Training and techniques of play were significantly different from those he had been used to, and however hard he tried to adapt to the local style, he was often not picked for the Saturday afternoon matches, or was picked only as a substitute, for a brief period of play. Two years or so later, when he moved to a team in Woodstock, he felt, rightly or wrongly, that his play was even less appreciated, and though he was expected to attend all the practice sessions, he all too often had to spend Saturday afternoons on the sidelines. (Sometimes also he was out of action because of injury).

There was a famous occasion when he saved the championship match for his team against Bloxham at Oxford United ground, by kicking two goals, but even that did not seem to make a great deal of difference to the way the coaches regarded him. Perhaps he was too sensitive in his reactions to a more competitive football environment than he was used to in Australia, but the effect was that, very gradually, he came to devote more of his thought and energies to cricket, and less and less to football. Football became a means of keeping fit and alert for the cricket season. But this is to anticipate a later part of Tim's story.

During the early months of 1982 much of our energies were devoted to the search for a house. Every post brought more notices from estate agents, describing properties through euphemisms such as 'gives ample scope for redevelopment' (hasn't been touched for 50 years), or 'the living room is deceptively large' (the living room is an alcove off the kitchen). Looking for a house was an opportunity to explore the suburbs of Oxford and the surrounding villages in conditions of deep snow. Because Audrey needed a workshop to set up her pottery again, we soon began to concentrate on the villages, where there tended to be more space for less money and a greater likelihood of outhouses that could be converted for her needs.

Some 'desirable residences' did not merit a second look once seen from the road, but we investigated quite thoroughly eight or ten houses, learning much about the house market and the look of Oxfordshire in the process. We commissioned a survey on an ancient rambling farmhouse in a village south of Oxford, but the area was so damp and the smell from nearby farm silos so obnoxious that we thought better of it. One house in Oxford itself was a depressing wreck that had been occupied by squatters, another in a village included a huge workshop but was on a very main road, others were charming but too small or too inconveniently located, still others were anything but charming with similar disadvantages.

When we entered one moderate-sized house in a village north of Oxford, we found that it contained some 16,000 'Christian books', including over 600 bibles, some of great antiquity. The quite ancient occupier told us that he was secretary to a missionary society and had been collecting books on Christianity since 1940, when he began his collection as a schoolteacher in North Wales. As his wife opened an airing cupboard for us and revealed books but no linen, she sighed: 'my husband is obsessed with books'.

It was some weeks into the search when Audrey suggested that it might be worth investigating a house on one of the estate agents' lists that we had previously dismissed as too far from Oxford. It was called 'Glym Cottage' (from the River Glyme) and was located on the edge of the village of Wootton, two or three miles north of Woodstock, which itself is about eight miles north of Oxford. The area is not quite in the Cotswolds, but is just where the flat lands around Oxford are beginning to give way to more hilly country. One afternoon we decided to go and see it. As we drove round the block from our temporary home we encountered Tim returning, somewhat disconsolately, from school, and told him to get into the car because we were off to look at a house.

What we found was two old farm labourers' cottages knocked together, with a modern extension, all in Cotswold stone, on a long narrow ribbon of land between a field and the road out of Wootton to the north. It had been empty for a year, including the coldest winter for a long time, and plainly was not in good shape. But there was a separate garage which could easily be converted into a pottery, it was sufficiently far out of Oxford to be affordable, and had an individuality that most other places had lacked. There was some mould on the walls and part of the roof looked in need of repair, but we could imagine it as a place to make our home.

Tim wrote to either Stephen or Rob in Canberra that he had been returning home after a difficult day at school, and was feeling depressed, when 'Mum and Dad drove up and said: "jump in, we are going to look at a house." It was a house we would really be happy in and I felt so much more cheerful.'

Gradually winter gave way to spring and the cold, which had been such a shock to us, eased. It was not yet quite spring when the time came in late February for Kate to return to Canberra to resume her studies at the Canberra School of Music. On the way to Heathrow airport we passed a ghastly accident in which a Range Rover had skidded across the central reservation and two men had been killed, and also saw a multiple rear-end pile up on the way back. These were a tense backdrop to our parting with Kate, who was in effect leaving home for the first time, except that she could justifiably say that it was home and her family that was leaving her. We were all emotionally upset by the parting. When we got back home we talked with Tim about choice of school subjects, and possible careers.

One Sunday afternoon early in April I cycled to Glym Cottage (which we did not yet own but were about to) from Oxford, taking 51 minutes there and 48 minutes for the return. The garden was full of spring flowers and blossom. Much more needed to be done to the house than was evident from the surveyor's report, for instance when water was let back into the 'drained' central heating system it spurted out through 16 separate cracks.

Tim was given the upstairs room in the original cottage, dating apparently from the eighteenth century. His floorboards were found to be on top of an original floorboard layer which was now rotten, so that the whole lot had to be taken up (revealing where an old staircase had once been), and replaced. The room had a heavy black beam under a white painted ceiling of wooden boards, which continued down at a sharp angle to the wall on two sides. The walls were well over one foot thick and roughly plastered.

We finally moved in towards the end of May. Tim transferred from the Oxford Boys' School to the Marlborough School in Woodstock (the local comprehensive high school) after the half-term break in the summer term of 1982. He joined the county cricket side and began to play cricket for Combe, a nearby village. We acquired a black female kitten, whose birth Tim had seen at a friend's house in Oxford. Life, for Tim, was beginning to improve.

In July I went off on a one-month trip, first to a conference on Japan at the Hebrew University of Jerusalem, then a day and a night in Athens in order to change planes, and finally to Japan for a research trip mainly in northern Honshū. I went to Israel with some apprehension as that country had recently invaded southern Lebanon in an effort to oust the PLO which had been shelling towns and villages around Qiryat Shemona. The visit turned out to be fascinating. On the day after the conference finished, a number of us were taken by car from Jerusalem through Jericho up to the Sea of Galilee, and to the northern border of Israel. There we picked up an army guide, and went into Lebanon as far as the Beaufort Castle, the old Crusader castle which had been captured by Israeli forces from the PLO three weeks before.

It was the first time I had been in a war zone and felt very mixed emotions about this particular war. Southern Lebanon was stunningly beautiful, but the lovely mountain landscape contrasted with the bomb-damaged houses and displaced families travelling along the roads past Israeli tanks in unregistered beat-up Mercedes. At this time Israel was going through a phase of euphoria that at last she was fighting a war outside her own borders, but the mood was soon to turn to one of disillusionment. If our car had strayed into a minefield, there would have been up to six vacancies in Japanese studies at universities around the world.

Tim wrote the following letter to me in Japan:
'Dear Dad,
Well at the moment we seem to be hearing alot about the war in Beirut and we hope that you got off safely to Athens.

Changing Country

Anyway, you should now be in Japan and I'd love to hear about what your doing in that strange country!

The amazing thing is, is that Brazil has been knocked out of the World Cup which amazes me. They were beaten by Italy of all teams and the four teams left now are Poland, Italy, France and Germany.

Today I didn't go to school because half the day was on a sports carnival and I wasn't in any of the races. My races are on Thursday and I'm in lots of sprints. So I just worked on the garden with the new "Strimmer" that mum bought which is really good.

On Sunday, Mum and I went to Cheltenham for a county cricket match that I played in. I got 60 runs which pleased me and I also kept well too (wicket keep!) Lately I have been so tired and nothing has really happened so it has been the usual boring time.

I am already missing you and I'm already thinking about when you get back. I have done up my room now that Rupe is outside and it looks really good. I've put up lots of Australian posters and it looks much better.

I know you haven't forgotten about the electronic game and Walkman etc. But do remember, I want a Walkman Radio and Jane wants a Walkman Cassette which will cost a bit more. I'm hoping the game is still popular so you will have no trouble finding the right one.

Do write soon, sorry it's so short

love Tim

P.S. Sorry about the writing, I know its deteriorating.

PP.S The pussy (Norm) is getting giant.'

I have not attempted to correct Tim's spelling, expression or punctuation. One thing that was to correct itself was the name of the cat. Happily the name 'Norm' was soon forgotten, and for a considerable time the cat, which in any case was female, appeared to have no name whatsover.

8 Trying Not To Be English

On 31 December 1982 I wrote a note at the end of the year's diary, which read: 'The end of the year, and a monumental year. New job, new house, new schools, new friends. Still sad though about leaving Australia.' At that point Australia was very much in all our minds and the boys in particular were determined to assert their Australian attachment. Rupert, who now had his room in an outhouse apart from the main house, covered his walls with maps of Australia, photos of Canberra, pictures of Australian animals, souvenirs of his Canberra school environment and so on. Gradually and almost imperceptibly over several years these tended to give way to more contemporary images of motor bikes, English friends and European trees.

Tim likewise decorated his walls with Australian maps and pictures of animals. He had a stunning print of a Tasmanian devil, teeth bared in a gesture of defiance, though as the caption from the Tasmanian Museum and Art Gallery pointed out, the animal was only 50 cm long. From the same source were equally beautiful prints of a forester kangaroo and a common wombat, and there was also a large mounted colour photograph, taken at night with a flash, of a sugar glider - one of the smaller marsupials - among the long narrow leaves of a eucalyptus branch. Although the maps eventually made way for book shelving, the pictures were never taken down, nor was the triangular bumper sticker with a representation of the Australian flag and the message 'Advance Australia', which decorated his clothes cupboard.

Gradually, it is true, other images appeared: the cricket and football teams in which he was now playing, girlfriends, and a magnificent poster of Suzanne Vega, who was to become his favourite female singer. To his collection of sports trophies from Australia was added a growing collection of ones from Oxfordshire. Scarcely Australian, but transported from the ceiling above his bed in Canberra to the ceiling above his bed in Wootton, was a large-scale poster of the control panels in Concorde's cockpit. That also remained through growing up and changes in interest and environment.

In August 1982 we did what in retrospect seems like an extremely English middle class intellectual thing to do by renting a house in the Dordogne area of central France. We had not visited France for many years and had little idea of the Dordogne's popularity with a certain class of English person, until we noticed the number of British-registered Volvos in the vicinity of Les Eyzies de Tayac. The house, which was unpretentious, was in the village of Berbiguières, not far from Les Eyzies. The quality of light on pink and brown houses and on the hills, cliffs and medieval chateaux of the region captured us for ever.

I was able to trace the family I had stayed with for six weeks or so when I was 16 in the Armagnac region and found that the boy I had exchanged with all those years ago was now a top surgeon in Paris. We called in on François and his family on our way home, though with little time to spare because we had been held up in holiday traffic and were in danger of missing the boat at Le Havre. We did catch it, however, and the moment we reached home again, Rupert and Tim went to the back of the car and pulled off the GB sticker, declaring that they had been wanting to do that all the holiday.

For Tim, the experience of being in France was partly new and partly reminiscent of Australia. When he returned to school after the holidays he was asked to write an essay on his principal memories of what he had done since the previous term. The notes for this essay contained nine items *(all sic):*

1) Canoeing down the 'Dordorgne' in France. Went with family for about 10k past Castle.

2) Sun-baking like old times. By the river with sun just like Australia.

3) Playing cricket at Oxford School of Sport. Learning alot!

4) French Food. Gorgeous baskets of Bread and great Patisseries etc.

5) Understanding French. Difficult but great fun.

6) Was given personal WALKMAN stereo and listened on the way down to Dordorgne.

7) Went to 'Madame Tussuards' in London and saw Dame Edna.

8) The great French Atmosphere; people everywhere, lively.

9) Pakistan nearly turned the tables in test, great excitement.

Test matches were always for Tim, not only a matter of intense interest, but also an occasion for competitive banter with his friends. So far as I am aware, he never even moved in the direction of shifting his primary loyalty from the Australian to the English team. In those early days, however, he even went to the extreme of supporting any team that happened to be playing England at a particular time. On this occasion there was a test series between England and Pakistan, and Tim, who in Australia had been an admirer of players such as Javed Miandad, sang the praises of the Pakistani team among his friends. It is a little surprising to me that he was able to get away with this provocation without alienating them, but it seems to have been taken as a mere Australian eccentricity, or just as Tim being Tim.

If Tim never lost his love for Australia, he was already beginning to accumulate experiences which made him realise that there were things of interest in the country he had perforce moved to. In November 1982 he wrote a letter to his friend Stephen in Canberra. It was not in fact a real letter to Stephen but a school English exercise, designed to have him express his recent experiences and feelings about them in the form of a letter. (He may of course have sent an actual letter to Stephen along the same lines.) The 'letter' begins in typical Tim fashion by saying that he had just gone back to school and 'already I'm dreading the thought of a whole nother[sic] half term. I just wish I could be in Canberra having some fun.' But he then reported in positive terms about a trip Audrey had undertaken with him and Rupert to stay with her cousin Mick and family near Hadrian's Wall, stopping at a youth hostel at Ambleside in the Lake District on the way back. He compared the Lake District unfavourably with the mountains round Canberra, but the scarcely believable antiquity of Hadrian's Wall impressed him and he commented to Stephen, not without banality, that 'England is such a different place than Australia when it comes to History'.

In mid-December Tim spent a week with a party from his

school on the Gower Peninsula in South Wales, where he and his friends passed their time abseiling, caving and similar activities. At the beginning of January Audrey took the two boys, as well as Kate and her bassoonist friend Wendy, both over from Australia, up to Yorkshire, where they saw Ripon Cathedral, Jervaulx Abbey, Fountains Abbey, Aysgarth and other places, The weather was as wet as the north in winter can be, but they went walking over the hills behind the youth hostel at Aysgarth.

Nearer to home, Tim became familiar with the grounds of Blenheim Palace, the seat of the Duke of Marlborough at Woodstock. Asked to write about it at school, he found it both English and attractive, even if the measure of comparison was on TV. '...The bridge was set into the haze and it looked so graceful and quiet it reminded me of Brideshead Revisited. It looked so English, the trees were still and watching down on the lake like old grandfathers.' His teacher was glad he found it so beautiful.

He was even learning to enjoy the rigours of an English winter leavened by group activity in the form of school tree planting:

'It was a horrible cold morning but we were all raring to go. Mr F... (the man from the county tree scheme) and Mr A... explained on a black board how to dig and plant the tree. Everyone thought it would be easy. We all put on our old clothes and our Wellingtons and went out and watched Mr A... start the first tree. Mr R... (with his old flares on) also helped Mr A... Everyone began and my group was all set to go. Before we had got the cuttings of grass off the ground, all of us had freezing cold hands and wanted to go inside but we stuck at it, trying to keep up with all the other groups.

'Slowly we ground away making good progress when Mr R... came over and tried to tell us a joke. "If twenty men dug one hole, how many men would it take to dig half a hole", said Mr R... Before we knew it Andrew quickly said the answer. "No such thing as half a hole". Mr R... went back to his tree and tried to think of another... I lugged the 'stake banger' over to the hole and my friend (Nicky) and I banged in the stake. We got the tree in properly and put all the soil back in mixed with half a bag of peat. Our tree was called

'Prunus Praticus' (or something like that) and we were very proud of it. We all felt much better when the planting was finished and we all felt like a rest. Before we knew it Mr R... was over telling us where to dig the next hole! Over the day we had great fun and our group planted three trees. By the end of the day we were all really tired and were satisfied when our drenched wellingtons came off. We certainly enjoyed ourselves.'

Tim's likes and dislikes at this period were of a graphically physical nature, and English images, such as beech trees, were appearing alongside ones that presumably derived from Australia. In September 1983, when he was three months off fifteen, he wrote the following two verses, as part of an English exercise based on 'The Great Lover' by Rupert Brooke. The influence of the original on the first verse is strong, but the second is virtually pure Tim, with its earthy focus on disliked food and other irritations:

Those Great Things
A new car rolling out of a car wash wet and shiny
With a bright blue sky soaking in the sun.
The sparkling of lemonade on a tingling nose
And the strong crust of home made bread.
Grainy smooth wood.
A forest of beech trees with leaves in the wind
Then footprints in the dew.
Beautiful powdery ski snow.
After, soaking in a steaming bath on that freezing night.
Then drowning in fresh dry sheets after a long day.

I dread
Brown bananas
That liver ruining a steaming Sunday casserole.
Burnt sausages
The stale fishy smell of the fish market
In the drizzling damp cloudy rain.
The crunching and squelching of a snail under your bare foot
A brown stagnant pond
Hazy party cigarette smoke watering tired eyes.
Annoying moths and insects flickering under the light
Then squashing them on the morning newspaper.

Not all of Tim's impressions and experiences were of such an innocent and homely nature. Football violence was being much aired in the media, and with his passion for sport he constantly discussed it with his friends and also with us. He witnessed a few minor examples in Saturday afternoons spent at The Manor watching Oxford United. In March 1983 he wrote a lurid story on the subject, which ended: 'All [that] was left was a silent deserted pavement with blood dripping down into the gutter.' His teacher plaintively commented: 'Oh dear - all over a game'. When the AIDS scare became big news, perhaps a little later than this, it became a staple of conversation between Tim and his friends. Once he pronounced authoritatively to Audrey and me: 'You're past it, you don't need to worry, but we've got to face this thing'.

One night in the summer of 1983 Tim and Rupert discovered that even in the depths of rural Oxfordshire physical violence could come uncomfortably close to home. From time to time a motor rally would come past the house in the middle of the night, some weeks after householders along the route had been informed and asked whether they had any objection. The boys had a special dispensation to get up and watch it. The following account, which Tim wrote as a school essay, is, with one omission, exactly as they told the story to us the next day:

'My brother and I had heard that there was another raleigh [corrected to 'rally' in red ink] going by the house and there was no point trying to sleep through it because it was just too noisy. We went up to the top cross road to see the cars screech and slide around the corner. There were quite a few people up there all watching the glaring sets of lights screeching around the corner at 3 o'clock in the morning. It was good fun.

'Later on we went down to the bridge to see if they took off over the rise. We stayed down there for about half an hour watching the cars. One car actually hit the wall on the bridge and bounced back out onto the road

'Slowly we walked back up to the cross-roads and on the way up we saw what we thought was a raleigh *[sic]* car which accidently *[sic]* skimmed another car's headlight smashing the glass. It didn't look serious and both cars drove off.

'At the top of the cross roads two cars were parked and two men were trying to call the police. They were both very angry.

Suddenly we realized that they were the cars who had bumped into each other. They looked drunk but we continued to watch the raleigh *[sic]*. The two men started hurling abuse at each other and arguing about whose fault it was.

'One of the men walked over to his own car and looked at the damage to his headlight. "I don't believe this, he has ruined my headlight. I'm going to show him a thing or two", said the man in an angry voice.

'He got in his car and put his foot flat on the floor going across the road straight into the other man's bonnet. The damage was bad. It [had] looked as though the man had hurt his head from the jerk. The other man who was sitting in his car got out raging with fumes [*sic*] and fiercely put his fist through the man's window swearing loudly. Blood started dripping from his hand and the other man got out of his car.

'My brother and I thought it was time to leave because we were witnesses to what had happened. We raced home and I thought about it all night. I couldn't believe how two people could be so violent.

'The next morning my brother went up to the cross roads and the cars had gone. On the side of the road was shattered glass and there were small blood stains on the road.

'The whole thing gave me such a fright and at the time it made me shiver.' [teacher's comment: "I bet it did!"]

The one thing which Tim omitted from this account was that one of the men had his girlfriend with him whom he may have been trying to impress.

Tim found that he was able to mine his Australian background in writing essays and stories for school. Not long after he went to the Marlborough School he was given an assignment and he filled some 20 pages of a school exercise book with a story entitled 'The Aborigines Answer'. He described it in a 'book review' at the beginning as 'a story with humour and thrills and I think it would suit the ages from 10 - 15'. In outline, it told how Tim broke up from school for the Christmas (summer) holidays at the end of his primary school career in Canberra, and when he returned home found that his mother had booked a five-week holiday for Tim and his parents (the rest of the family seems to have been in Sydney) at Alice Springs in central Australia. He is upset because this means he will miss his cricket and the Christmas parties, but goes to consult Stephen, who is engrossed in a computer game '[which] as usual...was going very well'. Stephen reacts philosophically, and never lifting his eyes from the computer screen remarks that 'it could be fun, there might even be some good birds up there too!'

'As you probably don't know', the story continues, 'Alice Springs is a very long way from Canberra and it takes about 3½ hours in a plane to get there.' In actual fact, Tim had never been to central Australia, but a few weeks before we left Canberra, in November 1981, Audrey had gone on a safari tour to Alice Springs, Ayers Rock, King's Canyon and other places of extraordinary remoteness, travelling in a rugged and versatile vehicle through sparse vegetation in burnt red soil where the horizon is refracted through the fiercely shimmering heat. At night by contrast it was near freezing and they slept well wrapped up in sleeping bags under the stars. Tim absorbed Audrey's vivid impressions of central Australia which she gave us on the memorable evening of her return.

The story goes on to describe the arrangements that had to be made for care in our absence of the menagerie of cats, lizards and rabbits. A scene of family departure chaos and bickering cuts to Audrey getting away with baggage eight kilos overweight at the airport, and then to Tim making up to the hostesses on the plane. At the hotel in Alice Springs we find the booking has not come through and I lose my temper with the management, but we are allocated space in any case. We meet a family called Atkinson, which includes a boy (Bruce) of about Tim's age. Audrey tells Tim that the Atkinsons (who appear to be imaginary) are going to take him with them to Ayers Rock for a week. He is not quite sure what to make of this and is prey to doubts and anxieties:

'I sat on my bed thinking of the week ahead of me, I wasn't sure what it would be like, and I was a bit scared at the same time. "What would happen if I fell off the great rock?" I said to myself. "And what about these Atkinson people, it seems a bit strange to be invited out with them after only knowing them for a few hours, even though they did seem very nice people, you never know they could be kidnappers or something. Oh Shut up, Tim," I said to myself, "I'm talking

Story of Tim

a load of rubbish".'

The Atkinsons and Tim travel to Ayers Rock in a Range Rover, which 'looks a so it had done a few long journeys in its time'. They climb the Rock, and later the two boys explore caves at the foot of the Rock containing Aboriginal paintings. Tim finds a piece of rock with 'strange writing' on it, which they take to a local Aboriginal who interprets it as directions for finding gold in a boulder at the Olgas (a range of humped mountains some 20 miles from Ayers Rock). Thereafter the story becomes predictable, and after a long hunt at the foot of the Olgas, on the very point of giving up and going home, Tim finds the right boulder and uncovers the gold. The story ends: 'We all were just standing there and crying our eyes out'.

9 Pond Life, Drums, Drama and Village Cricket

The telephone, for Tim, was one of the key necessities of life. I was well aware of his obsession with this instrument of communication because it was down a short flight of stairs from my study, and despite there being doors at the top and bottom of the stairs, whenever Tim was on the telephone downstairs, I could hear a good part of his side of the conversation. His room was next to my study, so that the most direct route for him to the telephone was through the study, in one door and out through the door onto the stairs. It was Tim's style to race through with a great banging of doors, often leaving both of them open, but this became a matter of confrontation between us, and gradually he came to realise that he would have a quieter life with less stick from his father if he moved through with some semblance of decorum, closing the doors after him. Even so, he would always make a point of leaving them open if he was going down stairs to fetch something, intending shortly to return: 'I'm just about to come back, Dad, so keep your hair on'. I would then make a point of shutting the door myself, so that he would have to open it again on his way back, which infuriated him. Since his route to what we called the 'old bathroom' was also by way of my study, there was a good deal of verbal jousting between us, though at times it almost took on a ritual character.

He himself objected to his own room being used as a corridor by people going to the bathroom or by me going to my study. The design of the house was such that the only alternative was to go down one flight of stairs and climb up the other, which was very steep. At one stage, though this is probably a little ahead of our story, he barricaded the door between his room and the study with furniture, so that his room was no longer a thoroughfare. This meant that he himself had to take a long way round to reach the kitchen, or the telephone, or indeed the old bathroom, but he was prepared to pay the price. My study also thereby ceased to be used for sudden and precipitate transit. Eventually, though it existed for several weeks, Audrey, suffering from a bad back, put an end to the barricade because she objected to carrying washing down one flight of stairs and up another when it was possible to make the same journey without changing level.

In any case, the 'arrangement' of Tim's room inhibited easy crossing. Games, clothes, books, schoolwork and sports gear were always piled without apparent order all over the floor. Tim rarely used the same towel more than once, so that the floor of his room was normally covered with wet towels. Audrey once, in exasperation, picked them all up and deposited them in Tim's bed, much to his subsequent discomfort. Although with time he was to develop an inner sense of order in organising his various activities, he never gave up the practice of what might euphemistically be called 'filing on the floor'. Tim was at the same time both extraordinarily well organised and extraordinarily badly organised: badly, because with depressing frequency he was racing round the house creating hysteria as he went, looking for some item (of cricket gear, or some school instruction sheet) which he needed with amazing urgency; well, because he, in essentials, learned (not quickly, it is true) to allocate his time with notable effectiveness.

The telephone was Tim's lifeline to a wider world than the village. He had friends in the village, friends at school (in Woodstock, about two miles away), and friends elsewhere whom he had met through sport or in some other context. One was a fair-haired boy called Pete, who bore a striking resemblance to Tim, and shared his passion for cricket. Pete also taught Tim to play golf, and because they lived several miles apart, conducted exhaustive dialogues on the telephone over the years of their friendship. They were not at the same school, but first met at a county under-13s cricket trial at Temple Cowley (on the south-east side of Oxford), some time in the summer of 1982. On that occasion Tim dropped Pete at stumps. After the game, Pete, in his parents' car, noticed Tim standing at the bus stop, so they gave him a lift.

Another friend was Andy, who was at school with Tim, and

was similarly a cricket enthusiast. Pete remembers Tim and Andy together when Pete first met Tim at Temple Cowley. Through football Tim met a boy who lived in Woodstock, called Jon, who was also a keen rugby player. Pete, Andy and Jon were to become arguably Tim's closest male friends, though their friendships matured at varying rates and Tim was gregarious and had many friends through school and various activities.

Of the three boys Pete and Jon had quite contrasting personalities, which seemed to mirror the physical build of each. Pete was tall and rather thin, inclined to approach problems from a theoretical standpoint, not for nothing the son of mathematicians, a trifle cerebral, sometimes giving at least the appearance of preferring ideas to people, interested in politics and not unimpressed by left wing solutions to the problems of organising society. Jon, by contrast, was stocky and built for rugby and thought few things more delightful than an evening with the lads after a rugger match. He was not unintellectual, but found life as it was naturally ordered more or less to his taste, and was therefore rather less interested in politics.

Andy was a more complex personality and harder to characterise, but all three from their differing standpoints had an intense commitment to sport, to music, to social interaction, to learning new things, and to cramming as much activity as possible into each day that passed. Tim never required his friends to be the same as each other, and had an almost chameleon-like quality of adapting to the character and interests of the particular friend he was with at a given time. So with Pete he would be intellectual and with Jon he would be 'ladsy', though this was all within the framework of broadly common interests and outlook that bound them all loosely together.

The chameleon element in Tim was perhaps a strategy with which to resolve a tension within himself between his sporting and other 'leisure' interests on the one hand, and a combination of intellectual enquiry and personal career ambition on the other. This is brought out in an exercise he carried out while he was still at the Marlborough School (the date is uncertain, but he was probably 16 at the time). He was asked to give an account of the most important ways in which his outlook on life was different from that of his parents. His essay was heavily annotated by his teacher:

'It is seven o'clock and the door of my house opens as my father comes in after a long and interesting day at work. First he kisses my mother and briefly acknowledges that I am present. My eyes are attached to the lighthearted television programme [teacher's comment: *name*] and *[when]* suddenly the television is changed to "Channel Four News" as my father settles into a chair. Did he enquire first? Yes, but still that doesn't make any difference! My mother wanders in from the kitchen as Margaret Thatcher is being discussed on the screen. *[Is it M.T. or her policies which are being discussed?]* "Just look at that woman, she makes me feel sicker *[more sick]* every time I see her", she says without much prior thought. We all start eating the meal and the routine continues most days of the week. What do I think about my parents' views on life? The main discussion areas *[can you have an area of judgement?]* are of course politics, education, leisure and most of all, general moral judgements.

'My father's outlook on politics is what I would call just left of centre... My mother I find is very similar... However she is generally not as interested in politics as my father. My views about politics are still very undecided and I like to think that I have an open mind on the *[entire]* subject.

'Both my parents got *[awful word]* good state education' (this was not entirely true) 'and both went to university. On this topic they also have set views and generally feel that going to university is the best thing. I think at the moment I would like to go to university but I am sure this is from influence of my parents. It's never really occurred to me that in a short time I could be out looking for a job. My parents seem to feel that university opens out a career in better jobs but my views differ in that you might spend many years at university and when you finish you still aren't guaranteed of *[sic]* the job you would like. *[ugh! be objective]*

'My parents also share different views to *[from]* me when concerned with leisure. Often, I honestly think that I could stop coming to school one day and want to never work again if I had some way of getting *[!]* money. If this was *[sic]* for

Rupert and Tim, Canberra, 1970

Tim and the Sydney skyline from Taronga Park Zoo, January 1972

The family at Seal Bay, Kangaroo Island, South Australia, January 1977. L-R: Kate, Jane, Tim, Rupert

At home in Canberra, January 1973; L-R: Tim, Rupert, Jane, Kate

'White sheep of the family': Tim in his Japanese kindergarten, May 1974

Tim on the beach at Bermagui, New South Wales, May 1979

Tim at home in Canberra in cricket gear, May 1979

The family at home in Wootton for our silver wedding anniversary, 30 January 1985

Tim and Alison near Les Eyzies de Tayac, France, August 1985

Tim playing hockey for MCS 2nd XI, March 1987

Tim wicket keeping for MCS 1st XI, summer 1987

The MCS 1st XI, 1987 (this was substantially the team that went to Zimbabwe). Photo by A.N. Middleton

Tim, Jon and the charred remains of Tim's bat, July 1987. Photo courtesy Oxford and County Newspapers. **Inset:** *Tim after delivering his A-level project to the house of his geography master at the last possible moment, March 1987*

Tim and Anna Jo before the MCS ball, July 1987

Tim batting for Oxfordshire Colts against Buckinghamshire Young Amateurs, August 1987. (Photo courtesy Oxford and County Newspapers)

my father I'm sure he would soon be a nervous wreck! This also applies to my mother. *[Why not say both parents here?]* They both enjoy working very hard and have very little leisure time. I couldn't live like this; I need to be either playing sport or relaxing in some way for me to enjoy life. When my parents do stop their work we go on holiday. They both like seeing historical monuments and general*[ly]* doing cultural activities. I prefer physical activities.'

He went on to discuss what he saw as our concern with the danger of nuclear war, which he shared, as well as sex and abortion, where he felt he didn't know enough about our views, but on abortion he thought we might oppose it in theory but not if a decision had to be taken in practice. He wondered whether we had boyfriends and girlfriends at his age, what they were like and what we got up to. Finally, he concluded:

'Basically for the future I would like to get *[!]* rich! My parents would call me a capitalist and I wouldn't disagree! Many people often say I look like my father and think I will turn out a very similar person to him. That thought I dare not dream about but at the back of my mind I think they might be right! *[after all there are bound to be certain characteristics]* One thing for sure is my views would have to face some widespread adjustments!'

If Tim's perception of his parents was infused by his own involvement in the family and search for his own manageable path in life, his view of teachers was sharply objective, well observed and not without sophistication. In December 1984 he was asked to write an essay on what makes a good teacher. Following introductory remarks about 'born teachers' and 'trained teachers', and about the importance of experience, he addressed the question of a teacher's appearance:

'When a teacher walks in to a class full of children knew *[new]* to him, he or she must give a general impression to the class that is of confidence and ready to take command of the class and really teach them well. ...Another point to remember, is when a teacher meets knew*[new]* pupils, he or she must let the students have a fresh start and give them a chance to impress them, regardless of previous reports from the teacher before.'

He went on to discuss specialist competence, and wrote that

a teacher should know his subject and the standards pupils need to fulfil, and continued:

'I know some teachers who are not geniuses at their subject but are excellent at teaching and therefore make up for this slight lack of knowledge. It is important that the teacher can give good help to the student and if necessary spend extra time making the student understand something. Also the teacher must be able to answer questions from pupils even though every pupil might ask a similar question but in a different way. I find this especially necessary in science subjects.'

On class control, he wrote: 'The thing that teachers are often noted for most is their control over a class. Some teachers I know can just walk in to a class and get attention and silence straight away but their *[sic]* are others that can't get pupils quiet and listening to what they have to say. The teacher must demand attention from everyone. If someone doesn't want to work that shouldn't worry the teacher too much as long as they are quiet and not disturbing others. A thing I find annoying is that some teachers make such a fuss over such trivial petty things and waiste*[waste]* time doing this. I feel the teacher should be quite strict and I don't think pupils mind this as long as the teacher shows understanding and will listen to pupils' opinions.'

He concluded that above all teachers should be themselves and have feelings like normal people, try to develop close understanding with their pupils, 'and if necessary try and *[to]* solve problems the pupil may have at home or with girlfriends and boyfriends. ... Most of all, I think the teacher pupil relationship is like *[just like]* a deal. They both have to feed in their work and attention and will get out of it *[and so will reap]* satisfaction and good work.'

By the school year 1984-5 (and indeed already during the previous school year), the serious matter of public exams was looming. In the summer term of 1985 he had to take a variety of subjects for public examinations, namely O-levels and CSEs. Part of the assessment for the CSE subject 'Rural Sciences' was by a long-term project. The pupils were paired off and with the help of their teacher chose a subject for the project. Tim was paired with a boy called Thomas, and they began work in May 1984. The topic was about bacterial life in four ponds in rural Oxfordshire. Unfortunately the final project seems not to have survived, but Tim's running notes on what he and Thomas were doing give a good idea of their efforts.

A draft introductory paragraph explains that they were at first baffled about what direction to take, but since they had done work on moulds in their third year, this might provide a possible subject of research. With the help of their science teacher they embarked upon a year-long study of bacterial life in various water conditions.

They chose four water locations, two being stagnant ponds (both at the school) and two being watercourses which flowed to a greater or lesser extent. Of the latter, one was a 'ditch' at Yarnton, on the road towards Oxford, and the other a place on a small river called the Dorn, not far from our own village of Wootton. Regularly every month they took samples of the water and tested their bacteria content, took air and water temperatures, measured the depth of water and recorded monthly rainfall. They had to take samples of the water in small bottles and durham tubes which were sterilised in an autoclave. The contents were referred to as 'McConkey broth', and a procedure was followed to test for the acid and gas content of each sample. This in turn gave a measure of the bacteria content. They also took photographs of the water at each site every month. On two occasions there was no result: at Yarnton in August because the ditch had dried up completely and in January the front school pond could not be measured because it had frozen to a considerable depth.

The completed project contained numerous graphs which displayed the results collected together in different ways, as well as photographs at appropriate places. They were able to make conclusions correlating various levels of bacterial pollution to different seasonal and environmental conditions. The care they took over the project was remarkable and Tim's notebook gives ample evidence of how meticulously they were being trained not only in techniques of analysis, but also to organise and set out their material, including an introduction and conclusion, acknowledgements, references, and what was described as a 'mini-essay describing my retrospective views'. In his draft of this last, Tim graphically revealed his enthusiasm, writing that: 'I have never been so proud of my work before, and Thomas and I [have been] very fussy about keeping the project clean and tidy'. My own chief memory of the project is of driving him on several occasions, together with his paraphernalia of camera and collecting bottles, the rounds of his water sites.

Indeed, at this period, which was before Tim could drive, the 'parent as taxi-driver' syndrome predominated. Audrey and I were frequently called on to drive him to sporting, social and school-related activities. Nevertheless, the lack of 'wheels' frustrated him and tended to confine his activities to the village and nearby places, particularly Woodstock. The village had an active youth club, where Tim would attend discos, and where he also quickly became accomplished at darts. (He also had a dartboard set up on the back of a door at home, and attempted, with little success, to raise me to something like his standard.)

In September 1984 he acquired his first real girlfriend, Alison, whom he began to take out after a toga party at the Wootton village hall, where everybody was dressed in sheets. He knew Alison already from school and the youth club, and their relationship lasted for nearly 18 months. They often did their homework together at each other's houses, where Alison would test him on his German vocabulary, although she did not know any German. They also read aloud to each other passages from the English literature they were doing at school, including *The Great Gatsby*, which was always a favourite with Tim. Alison taught him the Lord's Prayer walking round Oxford, since Tim was embarrassed that he did not know it. Alison, who was brought up a Roman Catholic, knew that he was not inclined to religion, while she herself did not believe in pushing her religion onto other people.

On a rather less elevated level they saw together the film *Morons from Outer Space* and similar productions. They also went to see *The Killing Fields*, about the Cambodian holocaust, which upset Alison, though she found it compelling, and Tim was touched to see that it made her cry. Audrey took them to see *Of Mice and Men* once in London, as it was a set book for English.

Given that my study was adjacent to his bedroom, I was only too aware of Tim's interest in contemporary pop music.

When the stereo went on at high volume as I was trying to concentrate on some student essay, Tim would be treated to a paternal invocation along the lines of 'Turn that bloody noise down!'. In fact, some of his tapes I could cope with quite well, but never any of them at the ghetto-blasting volume that he and his friends favoured.

He was a tireless propagandist for the Australian group Midnight Oil (and other Australian groups), as well as the New Zealand group Split Enz. His Australasian chauvinism, however, did not exclude music from the British Isles, and he was particularly fond of U2, from Ireland, and The Cure, from Britain. Suzanne Vega, who was to be a favourite later on, had not yet made an appearance.

Tim's friends all agreed that he was hopeless at dancing, though he would always have a go. But drumming was another matter. While still in Australia, he had taken drum lessons. He had a good sense of rhythm and might well have made a good drummer if he had had the time to practise, but he was into far too many other things. Once he and Alison went to hear a group called Blue Velvet at the Exeter Hall in Kidlington (a more sophisticated location than the Wootton village hall), and Tim was particularly impressed with the drummer, who played a brilliant solo.

He had a drum kit at home, and nearly drove me distracted by practising on the other side of my study wall. He played in a local band which met in Burditch Hall next to the village playing field and which was organised by Ann who also ran the youth club. One evening a week the drum kit, consisting of a side-drum, kettle drum, snare drum, top hat and cymbals, was loaded into the back of the car and driven the short distance up to where the band was to practise. Tim threw himself ardently into the band for a while, but eventually pressure of studying for exams and his increasing involvement in cricket squeezed drumming more or less out of his life, although later he planned to revive his interest in it at university.

While at the Marlborough School, he acted in two plays; *Oliver Twist*, in which he played Mr Sowerberry and the hangman, and *Oh, What a Lovely War*, in which he took no less than five separate parts. Tim's rendering of the Austrian secret policeman brought the house down. His powers of mimicry were appreciated by the master in charge of the play, who wrote on Tim's copy: 'a very good Australian German English Oxford accent'.

The village of Wootton is about half a mile to the east of the A34 (now the A44), the crowded but winding main road between Oxford and Stratford with a bad record for accidents. To reach the main road from the village means driving out of the valley of the Glyme which it straddles, up a steep and narrow hill between banks and high hedges, across elevated farming land to the A34. Directly across the main road there is Judd's Garage and to its right a pub called the Duke of Marlborough. On many occasions in the summer weekends Audrey or I would take Tim this way, then cross the A34 just north of the Duke of Marlborough and turn left along a road which first hugged the outer wall at the northern edge of the Blenheim estate, veered off towards the village of Stonesfield, and sharp left again to reach the village of Combe. The road took us through long established woods of beech and oak, past farm land and a farm which was much older than the woods, until we found ourselves in Combe suddenly, emerging from quite dense forest into some modern housing on the outskirts of an old Oxfordshire village of a few hundred people.

The car would be overcrowded with Tim's cricket gear and we would head for the unpretentious cricket ground at one end of the village. The pitch was noticeably sloping, and its condition was not always exemplary, but the setting was like one's early imaginings of what English village cricket ought to be like. On one side of the ground was the village church, of similar vintage to that in Wootton, with perhaps six centuries of history. Nearby were the old cottages and houses of Combe in grey Cotswold stone, the nearby village of Long Hanborough was visible in the distance, and the simple wooden clubhouse had photos of teams from decades back arrayed on its walls. It was a place to be savoured on a hot day in midsummer.

Tim played cricket for Combe perhaps largely because there was no effective team at Wootton and he wanted to play in a local team. The coach was congenial and his friends Pete and Andy also played. But apart from village cricket, he was playing county cricket from not long after our arrival in England. He was in the under-14 county side from around the time we

Village Cricket

moved from Oxford to Wootton. Although he had a bad patch in his cricket when he was 15-16, possibly related to the fact that he was rapidly putting on height, he was himself surprised to find that he was regarded as more than usually competent as batsman and wicket keeper.

Plainly, he had had a good start in Australia, where he was used to playing a full game of cricket, even when he was 11 or 12. Many of his English contemporaries had only experienced limited-over games. He also learnt to keep wicket in Australia at a much younger age than is normal in England, thus having a head start as a wicket keeper.

Probably Tim would have stayed on playing for Combe, but jumping ahead of our story a little, Pete in 1986 persuaded both Tim and Andy that if they really had ambitions in cricket they should leave the village side and aim at higher things. This led to Tim and Andy joining the Pressed Steel Fisher Cricket Club, part of the Cherwell League, whose standards were maintained at a higher level. Tim's own standards were rapidly to improve as a result. Even so, it took Pete, who by now was playing for Oxford Nondescripts, about two months to convince Tim and Andy that they ought to move, mainly because of their feelings of loyalty to their old club.

There was mounting evidence at home during this period that Tim was gradually becoming more and more serious about cricket. He would spend half an hour at a time 'knocking in' his bat with a cricket ball (not a quiet activity), while both the dining room and the living room were frequently used for practising shots (usually ball-less) with his bat. One day, which may have been a little later, I had a conversation with a West Indian graduate student at my College who played in one of the teams in the Cherwell League, and told me he was 'fanatical about cricket'. When I passed this on to Tim, he seems to have thought long and hard about it, even losing sleep overnight deciding whether he felt similarly. Eventually, he told us that he too had realised he was 'obsessed by cricket'.

There is still paint missing from a patch on the living room ceiling where Tim was practising a shot to the boundary.

In January 1984, Kate being over from Australia for Christmas, all six of us went skiing at Tignes in the French Alps, travelling overnight uncomfortably by coach there and back.

Story of Tim

The snow in the cold air was sparkling like a sea of diamonds as we tested our skills on runs of graded severity. One day I overbalanced at speed and fell violently face down in the snow, breaking my glasses which cut my face. Tim saw what had happened, and carefully guided me as I myopically groped my way down on skis back to the resort. There, the local doctor stitched and dressed the wound and I was able to ski again the next day. What remain of this incident are connections in the memory. The holiday as such was the last we would all spend away together, and we enjoyed each other's company.

10 A Change of Education

In the school year of 1984-5 Tim was for the first time facing a serious test of his academic capacities, which might also affect his future life chances. Having turned 16 at the end of 1984, he had to face his first public examinations less than half a year later.

During this period Tim was developing views on many matters, including what sort of a life he himself wanted to lead and what kind of a world he wanted to live in. So far as his own future was concerned, he was already of the opinion that in order to take part in all the activities he was interested in he would need to find himself a job that would earn him a great deal of money. At the same time, as is revealed in the essay which he wrote about his parents, he wanted to enjoy life in its many aspects, physical as well as intellectual, and the prospect of relentless hard work leaving little time for leisure activities did not attract him. Even so, he never seriously considered (though he may have talked about it once or twice) leaving school after O-levels and taking a job.

More and more, he came to see university as a necessary key to success, even though he did not relish the hard work it was likely to involve. When we were still in Australia his sister Kate identified him as the most competitive member of the family, and I remember a conversation with Tim when he was perhaps 14 or 15, in which he told me in that inelegant vernacular which he and his friends affected despite the protests of their parents: 'I intend to get to the top - right to the fucking top'. (In a similar vein, he once asked us provocatively whether we engaged in oral sex. To this Audrey replied with wonderful resourcefulness: 'Tim, that is an unanswerable question'.)

The 'getting rich' and 'getting to the top' ambitions which Tim often expressed might have been expected to lead him to take on attitudes which in Britain had come to be associated

Story of Tim

with the 'Yuppie' mentality. He was young and upwardly mobile and loved material things like good clothes. His concern with his personal appearance at times touched on the neurotic. He knew every type of car on the road and had views on the performance and attractiveness of all of them, especially those at the top end of the market. He wanted to travel and wanted a job that would allow him to do this.

Surprisingly, perhaps, these characteristics did not lead him into the kind of 'Yuppie' political attitudes which have been so often caricatured in Thatcherite Britain: wholly material values, worship of the market as the sole reliable allocator of resources, hostility to anything that could, even remotely, be described as 'socialist', authoritarian attitudes on unions and on law and order, tough pro-nuclear and last-ditch national sovereignty views on foreign policy. Tim was developing views very different from these although it would be wrong to describe him as very political; in 1984, the year of the great miners' strike, I do not remember him being especially worked up about the issues, though he was no supporter of the government's hard line. Politics for him was just one interest among many.

Still, Tim could be heard more and more expressing attitudes in support of the Labour Party, and he was deeply critical of Mrs Thatcher and her government. Pete, who was also somewhat inclined towards the left, explained it to me this way: 'In politics, Tim supported the Labour Party and was enthusiastic about his man Neil. I was not so impressed. Tim was the most honest bloke I ever met. He thought Mrs Thatcher was not down to earth and he absolutely abhorred her'. Certainly, Tim's dislike of the Prime Minister was visceral, and consistently held over a long period.

Even now, I am not entirely sure of the reasons for this. No doubt parental influence had something to do with it: he did not often hear praise for Margaret Thatcher or her government at home. Nevertheless, around the time of the 1983 election campaign, I had tried to instill into Tim a sense that, whatever one might think about her, as a politician she was not to be underestimated, and I think he probably came to accept that. As for his supporting the Labour Party, I myself - like many of my colleagues - had voted for the Alliance of Liberals and

Social Democrats at the 1983 general election (and again in 1987 before the whole enterprise was blown apart by internal squabbling - surely one of the stupidest fiascos of British politics).

Another part of the answer may lie in his Australian background. His life experiences had differed significantly from those of many of his friends, and his point of reference on many things was the memory of a society which he probably saw to be more open, with a more egalitarian ethic than that he was encountering in Britain. Then again, it may have been essentially a result of his temperament and approach to life. To quote Pete again: 'On music Tim was into lyrics in a big way. He was interested in them because he was interested in philosophy and attitudes to life. He enjoyed the fact that he didn't know, and he would laugh at the fact that he didn't know. He hated religious dogma. He was revolutionary in his own way. He was optimistic and would say: "if only people would do this and this and this...", whereupon I would reply: "but it won't work". In one way he was socialist, but he probably thought the Labour Party was more socialist than it is.'

During the 1984-5 school year, both Tim and we as his parents had to grapple with a problem that involved practical issues and also tested fundamental principles. The way in which it came to be resolved, through twists and reversals, shows the different and at times contradictory pressures which Tim was facing.

The school which Tim was attending was the local comprehensive in Woodstock. It had some excellent and imaginative teachers, and was run on lines which in many respects were progressive in the best sense. For instance, a number of disabled children, including some in wheelchairs, were accepted into the school, treated as absolutely equal members of the community, and helped to get around where necessary by their able-bodied friends. The concept of the school as a community was emphasised, and although the children were encouraged to study hard, some forms of competition, such as that involved in the provision of school prizes, were not permitted.

So far as public exams were concerned, however, there was

a problem, which became more evident as time went on. The headmaster was hostile to an 'élitist' exam preoccupation, and thought CSEs were a much better examination than O-levels. He maintained that the school had the exclusive right to decide what subjects at what levels each pupil should be entered for, and categorically refused to let us see comparative data on exam performance of his school by comparison with other Oxfordshire schools. Audrey, in high dudgeon over this refusal, went to the local education authority, which handed over the information without question.

Whatever the merits of CSEs the practical difficulty for a student aiming at university entrance was that a '1' in a CSE subject was seen as equivalent to a 'C' at O-level; in other words the best possible result was, from a university entrance point of view, unimpressive. The crunch came, in a sense, when the teacher in charge of 'Rural Studies', which was a CSE subject, tried to get permission to enter his pupils for a roughly equivalent O-level subject, 'Environmental Biology', and was met by a veto from the headmaster. Undoubtedly this caused disappointment and some demoralisation among the pupils, several of whom could have easily coped with the O-level exam.

Tim was entered for six O-level subjects and four CSEs. Two of the CSE entries (maths and chemistry) were subjects he was not wholly confident in and constituted 'double entries', whereby he might save himself by a good result in the CSE exam if he did badly in the exam for O-level.

Here again, it was Pete who set off a train of thinking in Tim's mind which ultimately led to an important change in his life, namely, to his leaving the Marlborough School after O-levels and moving to Magdalen College School, an academically inclined independent school in Oxford. Pete had himself moved from a comprehensive to an independent school somewhat earlier, rather in the face of his own (and probably also his parents') egalitarian convictions. As Pete described it to me: 'I had a similar experience in moving from Gosford Hill to Abingdon. I remember mentioning it while I was being given a lift in your car by Audrey and Tim. They both collapsed with laughter and continued to tease me about it. Most of my friends accepted it, but there were some who said "you think you're too good".'

According to Pete, the idea that Tim might consider transferring to MCS "started from one conversation when we were 14 or 15. I asked him what aspirations he had. ...With some surprise he said to me "you seem to think I'm bright". I told him I thought he was. He later talked with my Dad, who told him that if he wanted to go to Oxford he should take the Oxford Entrance. It took him a long time to make up his mind. Tim was more ambitious than most guys. He was worried about his career, and didn't want to spend his days sitting in some office. He was also worried about telling his friends at Marlborough that he was moving to a public school, but in the event he was honest with the guys at Marlborough and they didn't resent it.'

In December 1984 I wrote a letter to the Master (i.e. the headmaster) of Magdalen College School asking whether Tim might be considered for sixth-form entry. On 2 March I took Tim for an interview (where there was some doubt in my mind about who was interviewing whom), and in late March he received the offer of a place for the following September. This set in train an almost unbelievable process of agonising on the part of Tim, who acted as though he was being torn in two by having to making such a decision. Although we adopted a hands off attitude on the ground that this was a decision Tim had to make himself, it perhaps is not entirely honest to say that we did not try to influence him at all. Tim would probably have derived the general impression that I thought it might be preferable if he stayed where he was, whereas the emphasis of Audrey's discussion might have suggested to him, on balance, that he might be better off moving.

Some impression of the dilemma he felt he was faced with emerges from two A5 sheets in Tim's handwriting, one headed 'Magdalen School' and the other headed 'Marlborough School':

Magdalen School

Pros	*Cons*
Academic Advantage	Large FEES
Best Oxbridge entry	transport
Good stable teaching	Can't play football
Meet knew (*sic*) interesting people	A long Day
	School on Saturdays

Marlborough School

Pros	Cons
	Cricket
	Lose Marlborough friends
	BOYS only
No FEES	[blank]
Easy transport	
Free School Bus	
Small Classes	

It is noticeable that these 'pros and cons' were couched in practical, rather than ideological terms, but behind the practicalities lay, for Tim, both issues of principle and the question of whether he would really fit in to a school which he saw from a distance as not only highly academic but also more upper crust than he, an Australian, would feel comfortable with. Two other matters, not mentioned above, pointed in opposite directions: he was annoyed that he had not been allowed to take O-level in English literature at the Marlborough School; and he would not be able to do economics at A-level at MCS.

On 29 April, more than a month after the Master had written offering Tim a place and requesting a reply within seven days, I wrote him a diplomatically-worded letter declining the offer, but seeking to keep the matter open should Tim later change his mind. I cited 'the problem of Saturday school, the travelling distance from Wootton and the poor bus service, the danger of breaking with friends at the Marlborough School, the fact that he could not take economics for A-level at your school as he very much wants to do, and more positively his general satisfaction with the quality of teaching at Marlborough'. I delicately suggested that he was working very hard and was likely to do well in his O-levels and CSEs, and that the decision might have been different had it been possible to postpone a decision until after he finished his O-levels in June. The Master kindly responded that if 'either you or Timothy' had a change of mind after his O-levels were known in August, I should get in touch with him again 'to see if there might be a chance of fitting him in'.

In the event, he learned his CSE results just before we went

A Change of Education

on holiday in France in early August. He had obtained '1's in all four subjects he took, and breathed easily throughout the holiday. After we arrived back, however, and he learned his O-level results, he was less pleased with himself. He had an A in History, Bs in Geography, English and Maths, and Cs in Chemistry and German. As he well understood, these results did not bode particularly well for Oxford entrance, and the chance of moving to a more academic school began to strike him in a much more favourable light. I think it was probably about this time that he talked once more with Pete's parents, who took more or less the line with him that 'the system is iniquitous, but you might as well join them in order to beat them'. Tim realised he was underachieving in relation to his potential. As Pete put it, 'It was obvious to me that he worked more than anyone, and yet he didn't do particularly well in his O-levels'.

A bit over a year later, in what seems to have been an early draft for his UCCA (university entrance) form, he reflected on the Marlborough experience and why he had not done so well as he had expected. The writing was deliberately self-justificatory, and perhaps needs to be discounted a little: 'I feel very strongly about my rather mediocre O- level results. Firstly, what subjects I took was [*sic*] the most I could take, and I could [not?] take English lit, one of my strongest subjects. The exams along with strikes were taken without mock exams [Tim sometimes needed an interpreter: this apparently meant that some teaching was disrupted by teachers' strikes, and there were no mock exams because the headmaster disapproved of them.] and coming out of a continuous assessment Australian system, I feel I faired [*sic*] worse. (Also) lack of competition'. He added that he was setting his standards high academically, and wanted to attain a good university degree in geography. He had recently become fascinated by the philosophy of geography, arguments about different approaches and the future of the subject. He thought he had the right sort of personality for such an ambition: 'I don't always appear confident but inside I have an inner confidence which keeps me going'.

So, after a telephone call to the Master, I received on 30 August 1985 a letter inviting Tim for another interview at

Magdalen College School, followed by the offer of a place. This time I wrote in reply a letter of acceptance, and providentially Tim's paternal grandfather was persuaded to write a cheque for the required fees. Tim started at MCS on 10 September. For the first week he phoned Pete every night and told him 'they all look as if they ought to be on Blockbusters', and would say that nobody had spoken to him. But others agreed that he fitted in with little difficulty.

11   The Yellow Bullet

For Tim's elder sister, Kate, 1985 was a bad year. Late in 1984 she was diagnosed as having a muscle overuse injury in her right hand from her clarinet playing, and was ordered to rest the hand completely for a long period. This meant taking sick leave from her orchestral job in Melbourne, and not using the hand, which was exceedingly painful, for many activities such as opening tins and chopping vegetables. She was forbidden to drive a car and was supposed to have the hand strapped up. Kate and her boyfriend Simon came over from Australia for a few weeks at Christmas 1984, as did Jane and her fiancé Russell from South Africa where they were working at that time, Russell in a mining company and Jane as a pastry chef in a big Johannesburg hotel. A highlight of their visit was when the culinary resources of the family were mobilised to entertain to dinner one evening Prince Hiro, eldest son of the then Crown Prince of Japan, who was a graduate student at Oxford.

By the English summer of 1985 Kate's hand was still not better and she came over again to stay with us, taking a job for a while 'roguing' (eliminating weeds) at a nearby farm, using only her left hand. We took her with us when we went to France, as well as Tim and Alison. Perhaps the low point of that holiday was when we all shared two stifling rooms equipped with the world's bumpiest beds in a flea-pit of a hotel at Saumur, on the Loire. But we also spent absorbing hours at a *brocante* market at Duras near the Dordogne, saw the bison drawn by prehistoric men on the walls of the caves of Rouffignac, looked out from the battlements of the castle of Beynac over the river far below, and ate a sumptuous meal at a restaurant in Andernos, near Arcachon on the coast beyond Bordeaux, where Tim consumed a *demi-crabe* and I chose *anguilles persillade*. Tim and Alison spent a good many hours sunning themselves by a lake, and swimming lazily.

Towards the end of the year Kate, now back in Australia, had recovered sufficiently to rejoin her orchestra. Her hand went on to make a recovery so impressive, under inspired medical direction, that she even figured in an article in *The Lancet*. Jane and Russell got married at Wootton in December 1985, and shortly thereafter went to live in Mount Magnet, a remote mining town in Western Australia. Rupert had begun working for the University of Oxford on the trees in the University Parks, as the filling in his college sandwich course.

In the middle of September Tim and Alison rather formally (at a Chinese restaurant in Summertown, Oxford) celebrated the first anniversary of their going out together. But they were now at different schools and perhaps inevitably, drifting apart. One evening, Tim announced to us that he and Alison were not going to be seeing each other any more. When I asked him how he felt about that (in retrospect, an insensitive question), he snapped 'How do you think I feel?' and burst into tears. But within a week or two they were meeting again, and Tim was heard to say to one of his friends over the phone that it was perfectly acceptable to get back together with a girl so long as she had not told her friends about the split. In the event, they parted for good not long after Christmas, but this time, Tim took things much more calmly, realising perhaps that his life was moving into new directions.

One practical problem that faced Tim with his change of schools was how to find a reliable way of travelling the eleven miles or so from home in the country through the appalling rush hour traffic into Oxford and out beyond the centre of the city. Unlike what he had been used to, there was no school bus. The ordinary bus into Oxford left far too late in the morning. I could sometimes take him to school by car, but it doubled the time I normally took to get to work, and in any case I was quite often away. Tim had anticipated this as a difficulty and placed 'transport' in the deficit column when trying to decide whether to change to MCS or stay at the Marlborough School. He was still too young to drive. A solution came in the form of a boy called Tom, and a car of uncertain vintage called the 'Yellow Bullet'. Tom lived in a village a few miles further north than Wootton, and gave lifts by prearrangement to several of his friends needing to travel to school in Oxford. Shortly after he began at MCS, Tim was able to join this group.

I had occasion to remember the Yellow Bullet because one day it broke down irretrievably a few hundred yards past our house, and I had to drive all its occupants into Oxford. Often in the winter it was necessary to bump-start it down the hill on which it was parked. An MCS boy called Christian first met Tim on the first day that Tim travelled in the Yellow Bullet, and in retrospect was surprised he was on time. That morning Christian was in the back of the car and Tim was in the front, so that he could only see the back of Tim's head and found it difficult to gauge what Tim was really like. By the second morning they were quite relaxed and after two or three mornings it was as if they had known each other for weeks.

Philippa, an occasional Yellow Bullet traveller, has a vivid memory of the first day she met Tim. She was staying with Christian's sister Anna Jo for the weekend and on the Saturday morning Tom agreed to take them into town on his way to school. There was only Tom, Anna Jo, Christian and Philippa herself in the car, but she soon realised that they were picking up someone else when the car stopped outside a cottage in Wootton. They just sat there for five minutes and nothing happened. There were the odd comments such as 'Do you think he knows we're here?' and 'I bet the lazy **** is still in bed!!!' Eventually Tom rang the back door bell and as he was getting back into the car it flew open. Out rushed a boy with bright blond hair in a complete state! His hair was absolutely soaking wet, making it obvious that he had just got out of the shower, his tie was around his neck (but not done up) and he was carrying his bag and jacket in his hands. He jumped into the car panting his apologies and asking Tom to turn the radio on, all in one breath. It soon became clear that this was so that he could listen to the cricket results as Australia were playing at the time. Philippa gathered from the others that this was a fairly regular occurrence.

The Yellow Bullet seems to have been, among other things, a travelling debating society. One boy, Philip, preferred to make jokes rather than become bogged down in argument, but he tended to be 'crowded down' (Christian's phrase) by his friends who liked argument. Christian and Anna Jo's father was engaged in a campaign to stop a local disused airfield being a centre for microlites, as well as other kinds of development. His children supported him in that but Tom was inclined to argue that new development should be encouraged. According to Christian, Tim did not take sides in the argument, but added logical and thoughtful ideas, and wanted the argument to be nice and organised. He often went along with what a person was saying, but tried to produce give and take between the contestants, his own stance being one of neutrality. Of course Tim, as we know, could also be combative in argument if he felt deeply about something.

Despite some qualms in the first week or so, expressed at length on the phone to his local friends, Tim settled quickly into his new school environment. The buildings were completely unpretentious, and indeed the Master's office was in what appeared to have been a portable classroom. The atmosphere, however, was competitive, and he was expected to work extremely hard. He was soon advised that his German was too far behind for it to be worth while taking an A-level in it, and he soon shifted from German to English. For the next two years his academic energies had to be concentrated on geography, history and English.

The school also inherited aspects of the British public school tradition, in particular a system of houses, to one of which Tim was duly allocated. His reputation as a cricketer had preceded him and his housemaster had been talking about 'this amazing cricketer coming next term: the house is going to win everything!' Tim, with his determination to work out his own destiny for himself, now found himself up against a tough individual who had ideas for Tim which did not necessarily coincide with what he wanted for himself. In the words of Angus, one of Tim's friends, the housemaster was 'loopy about hockey'. After Christmas Tim, who had occasionally played hockey at his school in Woodstock, was recruited into the team and with his general sporting ability began to show real promise as a player. According to Christian, he played hockey much as he played cricket, with cover drives and back foot shots. He held the handle of the hockey stick lower than he should have done and had a stance as for cricket. Unfortunately, being shortsighted he insisted on wearing his glasses for the matches and on three successive occasions had them broken. On the third occasion he also sustained a black eye. Christian recalls the housemaster coming into the library, spotting Tim's black eye and commenting 'the girls will be impressed; you've beaten up a big bloke'.

Partly from having his glasses broken and partly because he wanted time to catch up on academic work during the winter in order to be able to concentrate on cricket in the summer, Tim decided that he had had enough of hockey and informed his housemaster to that effect. The housemaster was not prepared to accept a unilateral decision of this kind and things moved rapidly towards confrontation, with permission for Tim to attend a forthcoming cricket course being made dependent on his continuing to play hockey for his house. Tim, however, held his ground and there was a parental intervention in the shape of a letter to the Master (headmaster) from his mother protesting at the drain on the family exchequer which weekly replacements of glasses were causing. The fair-minded Christian suggested to Tim that it was strange for the teacher of a team to have someone who was good but who would not play, so why did he not give in? But Tim was in no such mood. In the end, after conciliation by the sports master and the involvement of the Master himself, Tim was allowed to drop hockey and to attend the cricket course. In the opinion of Tim's close friend Jon, his housemaster had a rather military approach, and took a tough line on hockey because he wanted to build Tim up. After this episode was resolved, relations between them became far more relaxed, he encouraged Tim in his cricket, made him a house prefect and later a school prefect.

Tim went on to order contact lenses, initiating a frantic morning and evening ritual of sterilising and fitting (or removing) these tiny objects which tied up the bathroom for long periods and nearly drove his family to distraction. One evening I was summoned to search for a lens which he thought had dropped out in the living room. We hunted high and low, with Tim becoming increasingly hysterical, no doubt (though I forget the details) because he had some appointment to go to. In the end he realised that it had somehow drifted behind his eye and he was able to retrieve it. Life at home with Tim was often a series of panics of this kind, not least over late essays for school.

Soon after he passed his seventeenth birthday in December 1985 he signed up for a series of driving lessons. For some considerable time I had been teaching him to drive our Mini on a back lane, with no traffic, not far from home, so he started with some advantage. Unlike his brother, he had never been particularly interested in motor bikes, or indeed in automotive maintenance, though he knew the make of, and often had strong opinions about, almost every car on the road.

After moving from Australia, both Audrey and I had had to take driving tests to obtain a British licence, and both of us (we knew how to drive, after all!) taking the process too lightly were failed on first attempt by a particularly dour Scots test examiner. Tim, after his course of lessons, was confident that he would do better than his parents and pass first time. Imagine then his chagrin when he was told he had failed and that the principal reason for his failure was that he had driven at 35 miles per hour along a 40 miles per hour road! As he told one of his friends: 'I was failed for going too slowly, what else?' Perhaps the examiner had sensed his over-confidence and decided that it would be safer to bring him down a peg on this occasion. He passed on the second attempt, which transformed his freedom and mobility, though it led to family arguments about who had the Mini.

Sometime in the spring or summer of 1986 Tim went on a geography excursion to Barton Cliffs in Hampshire, near the Dorset border. The purpose of the trip was to study the physical geography of the area, which had been affected by processes of rapid erosion. They went to Hurst Castle, and looked at the deposition patterns in Southampton Water, where material from the cliff line is moving down the spit. This is an area where man has interfered with natural processes by acting to protect the beaches. During the expedition there was, according to the geography master in charge, 'some activity not in the interests of knowledge'. When they were unloading the gear in the car park, Tim, whose interest in golf will be mentioned later, demonstrated a No. 5 iron shot with a measuring pole. Suddenly there was a loud crack and it was in two pieces. He went bright red, sincerely apologised, but then took the attitude 'now, let's get on with life'.

It was not, however, Tim's day. Shortly afterwards he put another measuring pole in the sea, it floated away and was lost. This was, however, a close group of boys, and in the understatement of the geography master, 'there were moments when they took things lightly'. The environment also impressed them. One of the party, Nick, remembers that the weather was wet, there were huge seas and there was a distant view of the Isle of Wight through a rainstorm.

12 Oxford Entrance

At the end of June 1986 I set out on a trip to Australia, Japan and Korea, finally returning to Britain in early October. I have a vivid memory of landing at an almost deserted Perth Airport at 3.15 in the morning, walking on Australian soil for the first time in four and a half years, and ordering breakfast in a cafeteria from the women behind the counter, who were so cheerfully Aussie that I suddenly and overwhelmingly felt I had come back home. This was followed by a stay with Jane and Russell in Mount Magnet, and then with Kate in Melbourne, eight weeks in Canberra doing research and a complex and memorable itinerary in Japan and Korea.

One result of being away through the summer was that I never set eyes on Anna, Tim's new girlfriend whom he met around this time. He had not had a girlfriend since breaking up with Alison at the beginning of the year, and according to Pete, they met at a rugby club party. Anna was vivacious and attractive, but not long after they met she went off to France as an *au pair* for six weeks, during which time they corresponded but could not meet. From shortly after she returned Tim decided that he needed to give all the time and concentration he could muster to preparation for the Oxford Entrance exams, which he was due to take in November. He therefore insisted on seeing Anna only one evening a week while he buried himself in work. His friends told him that this was not the best way to prepare for Oxford Entrance, and that he ought to see his girlfriend more often. She, meanwhile, was complaining to his friends that she was not able to see him. Eventually, after the exams, they met by chance in the street and after a talk decided to split up.

One evening, which could not have been long after I returned from overseas travel in October, I overheard from my study a long telephone call being made by Tim on the phone down the stairs. I could really only hear perhaps one word in five, but the conversation lasted for nearly an hour, I guess, and it seemed that Tim was becoming increasingly heated because he was under attack.

I learned very much later that the caller had been Pete, who later described this as 'the most major argument Tim and I ever had'. Pete thought that Tim had become over-involved with people at MCS who were too public school and spent all their time getting drunk, without really enjoying it either. Tim went through this phase and came out of it again, and in Pete's view it was perhaps natural as it coincided with the age at which one could be accepted in pubs and have transport. The rather more ascetic and cerebral Pete agreed with me that this was probably an example of the 'chameleon' in Tim; his tendency to adapt himself to the company he was in. For Pete it was this tendency which had fuelled the argument between the two of them.

It was Pete who had introduced Tim to golf, and induced him to join the North Oxford Golf Club. Tim's interest in it was always secondary to cricket, but he liked to take part in a variety of sports, so far as time would permit. As time went on he developed not inconsiderable skill, even to the extent of winning a junior trophy, though he was often frustrated that he lacked time to practise. In fact, it was a case of golf having jumped a generation. Although I had never played golf, nor developed any interest in it, Tim's paternal grandfather had been amateur champion of Warwickshire in 1931, so that he and Tim would talk golf whenever Tim visited him in Birmingham or spoke to him on the phone, though my father was by now in his eighties.

While I was away in the summer of 1986 Pete and Tim were allowed to take our main car (a Volvo of mature years) on a golfing trip to Scotland. Pete gave me the following account of the trip. They first drove up into Lancashire and stopped with Jane's in-laws in the town of Nelson. In the car they talked the entire time. Stopping in Nelson fuelled a discussion about north-south differences in Britain.

Tim had not really experienced the north before, and although he had met Pete's grandfather, who came from the north, he was not convinced by Pete's arguments that northerners were different from people in the south. He was struck

Story of Tim

by the hospitality they received in Nelson, but was not sure that this was something typical of the north. For many miles in the car they discussed whether it was that kind of a community that produced such hospitable people, or vice versa, that such people created that kind of community. It struck them how different was southern England as they knew it, where many people lived in villages in quite large houses, from the north, where the bulk of the population seemed to live on housing estates. They came to the provisional conclusion that the close-knit communities of the north, going back to the industrial revolution, though depressing to look at, must have produced the kind of people they had encountered there. These were hardly revolutionary insights, perhaps, but at least they showed analytical minds working from direct observation.

In Scotland they stayed at Troon and played, not at the Royal Troon, Royal Prestwick and Turnbury golf courses, but at other courses nearby that were cheaper. They boarded at a little guest house in 'Golf Place', within a hundred yards or so of three golf courses. The landlady was a little Scottish woman of about four foot ten inches tall, who because Tim was ill with a sore throat, brought him cups of chocolate. Despite feeling ill he insisted on playing 36 holes every day. His attitude was that they had gone to play golf and that was what they must do. When they returned to the guest house he would collapse on the bed, go to sleep for an hour, and even then he would still be out. On two evenings Pete ended up going out for a meal by himself because Tim was too ill to make it.

They drove into Ayr a couple of times and on their last evening after a good meal at a Chinese restaurant listened to rock music at a club called Shaw's. They gathered that the Scots took rock music much more seriously than the English. On their return journey they stayed with my oldest friend, John, and his family in Leeds. It was the first time Tim had heard grace spoken before a meal.

After I returned from my travels in October 1986 Tim told me with some enthusiasm that the Labour Party had just finished a particularly successful conference, which had affirmed a position of unilateral disarmament on nuclear weapons. I countered, mildly, that that probably would not do them much good at a general election given the gut feelings of the great British public. Tim's interest in politics was increasing and he was becoming more analytical about issues that concerned him. Apart from nuclear disarmament, he was concerned with equality, minorities, race problems and the Third World, but also issues such as the Channel Tunnel.

The prevailing ethos among his friends at school was small 'c' conservative, and he knew perfectly well that he was in a quite small minority. He had a kindred spirit in Pete, and though they were at different schools, they influenced each other a good deal. They had also both become accustomed to arguing for an unpopular line and being gadflies to the conservative majority. Pete told me that on one occasion in class at his school, taking part in a discussion on Russia, he had argued that Lenin had contributed more than Mrs Thatcher. He was met with incredulity as the others could not understand what he saw in 'this Bolshevik'. He discussed this later with Tim, who concurred with him, and they came to the agreed conclusion that Lenin had not been able to carry out what he wanted to achieve.

One friend of Tim at MCS who shared many of Tim's political views was Nick, who thought that though people saw Tim as 'a bit of a socialist', and though he voted Labour, he was not hard left, but rather a 'socialist-capitalist', who thought people should make money but not hoard it and should care for the less well off. Angus, who was more conservative, described him as a 'soggy socialist', but argued that whereas several of his friends tended to skate over political issues, Tim was intensely involved on certain questions most of which related to equalisation and connected with what he was doing in geography.

Informal debates on politics tended to turn into farce, as the left and the right would exaggerate their positions for debating effect and no doubt also from sheer *joie de vivre*. Tim was not immune to this tendency. According to Rupert (a schoolfriend), when Tim heard another boy, Stephen, attacking the Labour Party one day coming back from cricket, he asked him persistently for the reasons behind his attacks and countered with his own for supporting Labour. People sometimes became annoyed with Tim for probing their emotionally held positions in this way, but he was unusual in arguing that some things were wrong but not all.

On the other hand, when it came to be generally realised that he was passionately engaged in some causes dubbed 'left wing', his friends would deliberately provoke him into argument, and he easily rose to the bait. Once while in class, he was prompted by sceptical comments from a classmate to make a passionate defence of André Gunder Frank's radical analyses of Third World problems, leading his geography master to support him with the comment that one could not study the Third World and remain dispassionate.

Occasionally, others would touch a raw nerve in Tim. When he went with a school party on a skiing trip to Serre Chevalier in the French Alps at Easter 1986, and they met a group from a comprehensive, one boy kept referring to them as 'oiks from a comprehensive school'. At this Tim, with his own comprehensive school background, was outraged.

The most perceptive comment about Tim and politics was made to me by his main geography master, which I quote verbatim: 'In Tim's left wing positions there was at times some naive idealism. Sometimes he would be deliberately provocative, and at times he stepped beyond his brief. He was particularly liable to do this when historical matters were being discussed (the 'historicity of debate'), giving an opportunity for the historians to have a go at him. The political spectrum among sixth formers varies from year to year. In my experience most left wingers are theoretical, but I think that Tim was unusual in that he was a left winger who would actually have gone out and got his hands dirty.'

Tim voted for the first time in the general election of 1987, having become 18 the previous December. He set off for the voting station in the village hall with some excitement, but when he returned he seemed disappointed, saying 'voting doesn't seem such a big deal after all'.

Religion was hardly a major concern of Tim, although he liked singing hymns. However, where religion and politics or ethics intersected, he found issues that interested him. During his two years at MCS he was taught successively by two Chaplains, and came to be impressed by their intellectual sophistication. The first, who taught him in the Lower Sixth and the first term of the Upper Sixth, took them through Salinger's *The Catcher in the Rye*, which became one of his favourite novels, and he learned all the lessons that can be learned from it.

A new Chaplain, a much younger man, taught them in their final two terms and treated them in a liberal minded way as sixth formers. They started reading *The Screwtape Letters*, by C.S. Lewis, but when he asked them what they thought of it, Tim pronounced definitively: 'This is crap'. Jon also thought that it was a 'real turnoff'. The Chaplain said 'Fine', and gave it up forthwith. He told me that he had thought that they would be interested in the problem of evil as described by Lewis, but they found the book unexpectedly boring.

On one occasion he invited a vicar, whose parish was in a fairly working class area along the Cowley Road, to talk to the class. The vicar said at one point that he did not see how a caring Christian could vote Conservative. This brought a reaction from the class, but Tim was inclined to support him. The Chaplain remembers that Tim always sat next to the heater with his feet up on his desk (like some of the others, indeed), and when he came in, Tim would greet him in a hearty and friendly manner: 'here comes our great Chaplain'.

During the final months of 1986 Tim, as we have already seen, was preparing feverishly for his Oxford Entrance exams. Although at the end of his Lower Sixth year he toyed with the idea of applying to read history at Oxford, he had been fired by enthusiasm for geography, particularly human geography and within that especially issues relating to the Third World. The course in the Lower Sixth was focussed principally on physical geography, which Tim was prepared to work hard at, but it was when the focus moved more towards the human side that his interest really blossomed. He became greatly enthused by a book by Paul Harrison entitled *Inside the Third World*, which paid due attention to structural causes of impoverishment involving rich country policies.

His geography master did not initially rate the chances of Tim's getting into Oxford especially high, since when he first went to the school he only had limited writing skills, and his early essays were not good. His oral fluency, on the other hand, was much more impressive and no doubt helped him at the interviews, which were part of the examination process.

In the weeks before the examination, he had the bit between his teeth and worked like fury. Audrey and I observed this process and felt that he was spending too much time organising his notes and not enough time reading them.

He gave much thought to choice of college, and put as his first choice St Hugh's, formerly a women's college which was about to admit male students for the first time. According to Tim's calculations, this was a college with a strong reputation in geography, to which, not being one of the older colleges in central Oxford, it might prove easier to gain admission. He also had visited it at an open day in the summer and liked the atmosphere.

Apart from specialist papers in his chosen subject, geography, Tim had to take a general paper, which would consist of a choice of essay questions on a variety of topics. I remembered my own experience, three decades earlier, of taking a general paper, where on sitting down at a desk I was confronted with an instruction to spend three hours writing an essay on the following subject (no choice): 'Power'. Some instruction in the technique of answering general paper questions was given to Tim and his friends at school. In the days and weeks before the exams, he spent a good deal of time analysing past examination papers in an attempt to gauge the type of questions to expect.

I looked through the old papers as well, and noticed a preponderance of questions on ethical-legal issues of a more or less social nature. At that period Tim and I were frequently travelling in to Oxford together in the mornings, and apart from helping him with his geography revision, we discussed how he might answer questions on capital punishment, abortion law reform, the ethics of punishment in general and similar topics. This was a period when international terrorism was a subject of widespread concern, and I noticed that in recent papers there had been no questions on the ethics of terrorism. I pointed this out to Tim and suggested that he think about it as a topic. There was duly, as I had predicted (with no inside knowledge, I must add) a question on terrorism. This was the only time I was ever able to help Tim academically in such a direct way.

When the time came in November, Tim presented himself

at Oxford for the exams and interviews. He stayed for two days in St Hugh's and made friends with a number of other candidates from all over the country. In his application he had made clear that he wanted deferred entry, that is, he wanted to take a year off before going to university during which he would work for money and see the world. In the interview with the college geography tutor he said in reply to a question about what he planned to do in his year off, that among other things he hoped to work for some time in a ski resort. In response the tutor, a woman with a down-to-earth manner, asked him: 'Is this, Timothy, what I understand by the meaning of the term "ski bum"?'.

One morning, on 19 December, to be precise, I answered the telephone at work. It was Tim, but his voice sounded so strange - even hysterical - that my immediate thought was that some major disaster had taken place. 'Dad', he said, 'I'm in'. He had just received a telephoned offer from St Hugh's; in the jargon it was described as a 'two Es offer', meaning that he would be accepted provided only that he achieved a minimum pass in two subjects at A-level the next summer. His request for a year's deferment had also been granted.

The phone call from St Hugh's had pulled him out of bed, and shortly afterwards Audrey, whom he had picked up and whirled around in circles, heard him in the shower quite literally whooping with joy at all the opportunities this decision would open up for him, including, he very much hoped, eventually playing cricket for Oxford (one of his main reasons for applying to Oxford in the first place). He said to Audrey: 'I've got it all made, haven't I? Now it's all down to me to get it together'.

One of the friends he made staying at St Hugh's was Robert, who came from Shropshire. They exchanged letters for some time, and Robert, who was a committed Conservative, would end each letter with a provocatively expressed sentiment of enthusiasm for Thatcherism. Robert also obtained a conditional offer at the same college, and in one of his letters Tim wrote: '...it would be great if we could continue our lively discussion at St Hugh's while at the same time lighting up the JCR! On that subject, in my original letter I sarcastically ended up the letter by saying "socialism rules OK" but with acknowledgement of your sometimes flexible right wing views, I'll accept your opinion that they are only to provoke discussion. Some of my views also, I admit, are simply to do the same!'.

Tim also received, without interview, conditional offers from the London School of Economics and the University of Hull. In both cases the A-level conditions were tougher than those applied by Oxford, though they did not require a separate entrance examination, as Oxford did. Not only because of easier A-level conditions, he had no hesitation in accepting St Hugh's.

13 Race Relations in East Oxford, Landscape in Yorkshire

Following Tim's success, there were celebrations, no doubt wild at times, among him and his friends in the run-up to Christmas, including his eighteenth birthday dinner party. The sixth form had done unusually well that year, though one or two unexpectedly failed to land the offers they were hoping for. It was assumed by some that since Tim had received a 'two Es offer' he could now afford to relax, but when that was suggested to him Tim retorted that now the pressure was really on. If he did not do well at his A-levels in the coming summer, not only would St Hugh's be less than pleased with him, but he would fail to satisfy the standards that he was now developing for himself.

His chosen A-level subjects, as mentioned before, were geography, history and English. Part of the requirement for geography was an extended essay, based on some field research, which had to be handed in well in advance of the summer exams. After discussion with the geography staff, he embarked on what came to be entitled 'A study of the ethnic composition and distribution of minority groups in East Oxford'. What he sought to do was to examine the extent of residence concentration among Caribbean and Asian communities in East Oxford, and correlate this with socio-economic factors such as unemployment and housing conditions.

He used three types of data. The first was data from the 1981 census. This, however, was unsatisfactory for his purposes for three reasons: it was six years out of date, immigrants from the Caribbean and the Indian subcontinent etc were lumped together as 'New Commonwealth' (though there was a separate category for Pakistan), and only those born overseas, and not their British-born children, were identified separately from the 'native' community. He therefore needed to generate his own data, which he did by conducting a number of spot surveys at particular points in the district, including street corners and two of the gates of the Cowley car works, the purpose of which was to count numbers of passers-by under the categories of 'white', 'black' and 'brown'. He also estimated the proportion of 'ethnic' to 'non-ethnic' shops along the Cowley Road.

These on-the-spot surveys (with which his friend Jon gave him some research assistance) constituted the second type of data. The third type was obtained through interviews with officers from the Oxford City Council, the West Indian Community Service, the Indian Union, the Oxford Police and a West Indian friend of ours. He also made good use of the resources of the local history section of the Oxford City Library. He was advised not to attempt to interview members of the ethnic communities themselves, on the grounds that it was really too sensitive to allow a schoolboy to go interviewing people, some of whom might suspect that he was from the Social Security.

Given especially the inadequacies of the statistical and other data, the essay became a quite testing methodological exercise, involving the use of 'choropleth' maps of the area, and many tables of data and correlations between different kinds of data. In his Conclusion he felt that he had effectively established significant correlations between poor housing and unemployment on the one hand and concentrated ethnic populations on the other. But he recognised that the data did not sufficiently allow him to separate out Caribbean from Asian populations, an important reservation given their different cultural characteristics, nor did the data allow him adequately to establish the *degree* of correlation between the ethnic communities and the socio-economic conditions he was concerned with.

I vividly remember the circumstances in which the project was completed and handed in. Operating on the 'just in time' principle, Tim worked all hours that came in the week before the Sunday which was the absolute deadline for handing in. When I went to bed on the night before the deadline, he still had most of the text to copy out and finalise. By breakfast time, after working full tilt on it throughout the night, he still had not written his Conclusion. Since I had promised to drive him to the other side of Oxford to the house of his geography master where he had to deliver it by nine a.m. (as I remember), he had about half an hour to devise and write his Conclusion in the car. I was exhorted to drive with unusual smoothness so as not to upset his writing. At the house, some five minutes before the deadline, Tim found one of his friends seated at the dining-room table putting the finishing touches to *his* project. As Tim emerged from the house a few minutes later I took a photograph of what appeared to be a historic (or at least memorable) occasion.

When the examiner's comment became available, some months later, it read as follows: 'A great deal of effort expended in data collection, display and analysis. There was also an effort made to obtain primary data sources to complement and corroborate census evidence. He managed to identify some interesting relationships between factors which were sensibly and thoroughly discussed and analysed. However there was a marked overuse of Spearman's rank, which threw up a great number of redundant coefficients. Nevertheless, very much an 'A' class effort in terms of enterprise, enthusiasm and intellect.'

During the Easter holidays of 1987 Tim spent five or six days on a geography excursion to Settle in Yorkshire. The principal object of the trip was to study geomorphology and Tim, though his interest in physical geography was less than in the human side, developed a commitment to it when he was in the field. The party was looking at the impact of processes affecting carboniferous limestone, particularly the past glacial impact. Apart from geomorphology, however, Tim concerned himself with issues relating to national parks, and they spent a day interviewing local people about retail behaviour. Tim, gregarious as ever, enjoyed this.

Jon and Nick were both on this expedition, and their accounts indicate that, as with the Barton Cliffs excursion the previous year, there was plenty of levity as well as serious work. The master driving the minibus from Oxford to Settle found himself the object of groans and catcalls in respect of his driving. Jon and Tim would always pick faults with each others' driving, each accusing the other of passing another vehicle too close and so on. On this occasion it was the master who received their criticism.

The minibus had an unusual gearbox, so that when he put it into gear it would inadvertently lurch off into reverse. One thing which both Tim and Jon had been taught (and which Tim sometimes attacked me for doing) was to avoid making a noise with the ratchet when pulling on the handbrake. The ten or twelve of them in the minibus spent the journey up to Settle taking the mickey out of the master who was driving, shouting 'It's not a ratchet!' whenever he pulled on the handbrake and groaning when he missed a gear.

They stayed at a hotel where Jon and Tim shared a room containing a double bed and a single bed. Jon made sure that he got to the bedroom first and reserved the double bed. They took it in turns to have a bath, but once, when it was raining and very muddy, he did not wait his turn but made sure he had a bath first. One of Jon's memories of the room is that Tim's contact lenses and associated equipment were all over the place.

One night they hid one of the beds in a cupboard (Tim's according to Nick) and cleared a room so that its occupants would think that everything had been taken. In the course of doing this they managed to break a headboard of one of the beds. Thinking that a small headboard would be unlikely to be missed but that a broken one left behind would be noticed, they decided to take it away with them. Jon took all the screws and Tim brought the broken pieces of headboard back with him in the bottom of his case. They also tried to wake each other up by telephoning from one room to another in the middle of the night. No repercussions seem to have followed this less than exemplary behaviour.

14 The Heights of Cricket

It would be an exaggeration to say that Tim lived for cricket, even though, as we have seen, he had decided that he was obsessed by it. Perhaps, though I doubt that he knew the book, Tim would have agreed with the West Indian Marxist cricket writer C.L.R. James, when he wrote in his book *Beyond a Boundary*, 'What do they know of cricket, who only cricket know?'

Tim played a prodigious amount of cricket in the summer of 1986, as batsman and wicket keeper, but at least in terms of batting averages he did not shine, and was dissatisfied with his own performance. He nevertheless impressed a number of key people with his ability. During the season he participated in three separate teams, school, league and county, and how he ever found time for it all, and everything else, remains a mystery to me.

Although it was his first year at the school, he was made vice-captain of the 1st XI without anyone having seen him play, but purely on the strength of his reputation. The system was that the vice-captain became the captain the following year, but because they had not seen Tim play before the season began, the sports master reserved the right not to promote him to captain. He thus started in a rather unusual position and was under considerable pressure to perform. In fact he began rather shakily and only scored about 350 runs during the season, although this included three very good 50s. The team captain in 1986 was a phenomenal batsman, but did not show so much interest in organisation. Tim found he could take over much of the task of organising and managed to do this without antagonising the captain.

It will be recalled that Tim and his friend Andy, after long deliberation, moved from the village cricket environment of Combe to the more high powered and competitive Pressed Steel Fisher Cricket Club - part of the Cherwell League - in

Story of Tim

the spring of 1986. Michael, the Chairman of the Pressed Steel Fisher Club, recalls the first net practice in which he encountered Tim. When Tim batted he appeared very flashy outside off-stump and very back-footed, typically Australian where the ball leaves the wicket much faster than in England. Michael thinks that he probably had him caught at least four times in that session, but such was Tim's annoyance that he was never able to repeat that feat.

In June he broke through the barrier and was picked for the 1st XI in place of their regular wicket keeper, who was on holiday. He took his opportunity well, although he missed a difficult stumping, and made a smart catch from Michael's bowling. He was not required to bat, as they won without losing a wicket, but what amused their players who had not experienced Tim was his constant shouts from the pavilion steps of 'We'll have some of that!' each time another boundary was struck.

He was, incidentally, known at school as 'All over the shop Stockwin'. According to Angus, Tim was trying once to sell him a cracked bat, wouldn't accept that it was broken and said: 'only surface cracks; you can hit with it all over the shop'. When he or somebody else hit a good shot, he would say: 'Wooaaf, all over the shop!' According to Christian, he never held back, would use his gloves, clap, shout 'on your toes, everyone!', and would use Aussie slang: 'take a blow there!' or 'give it some tap!' (show what you're made of).

Tim had been involved in county cricket since not long after his arrival in Oxford, and played every year for the county team, usually captaining it, but in July 1986 he was admitted to the prestigious Colts team, which had an upper age limit of 19. Chris, who was organiser of the Colts side and also had responsibility for the County Cricket Association, remembered Tim from the colour of his hair and his large glasses, having once seen him play as a 13 or 14 year old. He had heard that he was a 'flash Aussie', but when Tim came to see him in the summer of 1986 he was anything but flash. He was surprised to be selected for the Colts and remained throughout that season slightly insecure as a cricketer. He attended various residential youth cricket training sessions throughout his teens, and at one point won through to the South of England trials.

Much to his disappointment he was not picked for the team, but he was competing against two other outstanding wicket keepers. In 1987 he was a reserve for the South of England versus The Rest.

Everyone agreed that by the 1987 season his cricket - and especially his batting - was transformed. In Chris's words, he came back in February 1987 looking a totally different player.

He was without difficulty made captain of the School 1st XI. In the words of his schoolfriend Rupert: 'his was a thinking captaincy, a pressure captaincy. He also tried to lead by example. Initially when he started being captain it didn't work out well. Other members of the team knew that he was a county player and therefore if he was dismissed it discouraged people. The rest of the team would then say: "what are we to do now?". Realising this, two or three games into the season, Tim told the team: "you can't just rely on me; everyone is capable of getting runs". So the pressure was lifted off Tim, and the best thing about the season from then on was that we played as a team.' According to his sports master, Tim was good at spotting when a player was beginning to lose concentration, and when he saw that somebody's game was deteriorating he would give encouragement. He did not simply criticise, which in such circumstances would have been counter-productive, but made positive and constructive comments.

The season did not start auspiciously for Tim, since in the game against Pangbourne College he was caught at square leg for a duck. But in 14 games he scored 108 not out against Douai School, 105 not out against Oratory School, 96 not out against Lord Williams School and 94 (caught from a pull shot to mid wicket) against the Old Waynfletes. He totalled 740 runs for the 14 matches, giving an average score of 67.3. Here was glory indeed, and Tim was in his element. The team played 15 matches (one of which Tim missed because of exams), won five, drew nine and lost one (against the MCC). Some of the drawn matches had to be abandoned because of rain.

This year Tim was selected for the Pressed Steel 1st XI for his batting, though because of other commitments he could not play until June. At a match in July against Swindon British Rail he was again asked to substitute as wicket keeper. The following story was told me by Michael about this match: Pressed Steel's best spin bowler was creating havoc moving the ball regularly past the bat. Each ball was accompanied by Tim going 'Oooh' and 'Aaah', much to the Swindon batsmen's annoyance. He was asked by a particularly edgy batsman to 'shut up', but to no avail. A quick single was taken, Tim and the batsman clashed as the ball was returned, dust flew, Tim collected the ball, and the batsman struck out at Tim with his bat. Michael had never seen so many of their players move so fast to defend a player. 'We'll have none of that behaviour here,' said the spin bowler, a man not known for avoiding trouble.

Tim remained in the 1st XI all season, and the team went on to win its last nine matches to finish runners up to Cowley St John. His last major contribution as a batsman was against North Oxford, where Pressed Steel needed 47 runs to win with Tim and another player batting. Not only did they score the required runs but Tim managed to upset the Oxfordshire County wicket keeper by taking singles when he fumbled the ball. 'There's a run to that old clown,' said Tim rather too loudly, though the wicket keeper was barely in his forties.

He also played for the Colts, and although he did not score sensationally, what the team achieved in 1987 was, in Chris's view, due substantially to him. In assessing Tim's cricketing ability, Chris was inclined to be sceptical about some rave assessments in the local press ('No Stopping Ton-Up Tim' was one headline). In his view he had real potential for county cricket but still had a long way to go. Sometimes still he lacked concentration and made indiscriminate shots, but on the other hand he had achieved enormous progress over the previous 12 months. This was echoed by his sports master, who thought that Tim was limited in his ability to dominate bowlers when conditions were other than ideal for batting. He had something of the 'Boycott temperament', maximising his runs in good conditions, but on the other hand he progressed tremendously during the season.

I should perhaps add that Tim was in no sense part of the Boycott fan club, and was frequently critical of him, believing that the individual ought to be willing to sacrifice his own glory for that of the team. He had, moreover, an extraordinary memory for shots. According to Pete, if somebody had bowled him out in a match two years before, he would remember the name of the bowler and exactly what type of a shot it was. He studied shots of top cricketers on TV, by watching test matches and so on and he talked quite frequently with top coaches in Oxford.

After the end of the 1987 season he was offered the captaincy of the Colts for the following year, which thoroughly delighted him.

He was delighted also with his personal good fortune from early April 1987, since he had not had a girlfriend after breaking up with Anna late the previous year. He now started going out with Anna Jo, who had been an occasional passenger in the Yellow Bullet the previous year, and who was the sister of Christian. In a mood of fatherly flippancy I suggested to him that at this rate of progression through the alphabet he would be fairly antiquated before he had a girlfriend called Zoë, but I am not sure that this was entirely appreciated.

Anna Jo and Tim soon found things went well between them, and since they were both at schools near the centre of Oxford, and lived in nearby villages, they were able to see each other frequently. During the earlier Yellow Bullet period, he had sometimes given her a hard time in argument. With some lack of consistency he would tell her he represented the ordinary man in the street and that she was from the monied classes attending an independent school. Once she asked him whether he knew that she had been at a state school for part of her education. 'What age did you leave it then?' asked Tim. 'Age eight', she replied. After this, she felt that she had lost the argument.

One of the first events Tim went to with Anna Jo was a point-to-point meeting. There is a photograph of him sitting on top of the Volvo watching the horses through binoculars. She attended some of the cricket matches he was playing in and found time for socialising in Oxford with their friends. Tim at this time was revising for his A-levels (insofar as cricket left him time for this) and had become absorbed in the poetry of Philip Larkin, among other modern poets, the novels of Thomas Hardy, some Shakespeare (particularly *Othello*), and Scott Fitzgerald's *The Great Gatsby,* most of which were on the syllabus for A-level English. Milton he found tougher going, but put in much work on it. He also had copious history notes to go through, not to speak of physical and human geography.

Anna Jo, whose A-levels were not till the following year, found it difficult to study alongside Tim, as he was always opening and shutting books, rustling papers, and throwing his pen down. Likewise shopping with Tim took an excess of time, since he had to find the best quality, the best deal, however long it might take. But discussion about everything under the sun was another matter. They also listened together to tapes of groups that one or other of them appreciated. My own understanding of or liking for pop music was strictly limited, but I could listen to tapes of a new star in Tim's and Anna Jo's musical firmament, Suzanne Vega, whose voice was quite haunting. Tim, and with him Anna Jo, were interested in lyrics, in other words, in what the singer actually said, and I agreed that with a singer such as Suzanne Vega the lyrics were indeed worth concentrating on. I happened to discover that she practised a Japanese religion, Nichiren Shōshū.

One morning, in the last week of of his final term at MCS, Audrey took a telephone call from Tim, who had been staying overnight with his cricket friends in the school pavilion. Hearing his opening gambit: 'Mum, absolute disaster! you'll never believe it', her first thought was that they had managed to set the pavilion on fire. In fact, what had happened was this: as captain of the school 1st XI Tim ran a fining system, whereby those who scored badly in a match would contribute towards a celebratory dinner at the end of term and of cricket week. The fund built up to about £40, with the help of which they went out to an Indian restaurant in the Cowley Road. On their return, following tradition, they slept in the pavilion, leaving Jon's car, containing Tim's cricket gear in the back, in the school car park. They were living it up rather, and someone was sick over the steps, but that was the extent of damage to the pavilion.

Next morning Jon's car had disappeared from the car park. They hoped that it was a joyrider who had taken it and that when it was found Tim's gear - not to speak of the car itself - would be intact. A few hours later the police took them to see it where it had been discovered in Blackbird Leys, an outer suburb. The car had been set alight and was completely gutted. The paint was burned off to the extent that it was difficult to tell what colour the car had been. Virtually the whole of Tim's cricket gear, contained in a large black box known as 'the coffin', was reduced to ashes.

For both Jon and Tim this was a great crisis. Jon had lost his car, which though old would be expensive to replace, as well as a certain amount of cricket equipment and tapes. Tim had lost the best bat he had ever had, and nearly all the rest of his gear. He had a Colts match the very next week, and other cricket fixtures, including the school tour to Zimbabwe, looming a little further off. The affair was reported in the local paper, alongside a photograph of Jon and Tim looking solemn and holding the charred remains of the bat. Tim had received most of his equipment from a sponsorship arrangement with a cricket gear manufacturing firm, but there was no question of them replacing it free of charge.

Soon afterwards, however, the father of an old boy of the school kindly and anonymously offered to replace the lost equipment. Tim and Jon went to a cricket suppliers in Cheltenham and replaced essentials, after which Tim order the bulk of the replacement gear from the firm that had sponsored him, in London. A few days later, Tim's teammates ceremonially but unceremoniously threw him into the River Cherwell, and he came up smelling of river slime.

A little earlier than this, Tim and Anna Jo went to the Magdalen College School Ball, a memorable occasion indeed. Tim had just returned from playing a cricket match, and, on sitting down to eat, Anna Jo instantly noticed that he had no cufflinks, and then Tim told her that his shirt was actually held together with sellotape. He had, incidentally, bought his dinner jacket and trousers for £15.00 at a market, and when Audrey pointed out that the trousers did not match the jacket, took the trousers back and was able to persuade the stallholder to exchange them for a pair that came closer to matching the jacket. To solve the problem of no cufflinks, they first tried to convert Anna Jo's earrings to an unorthodox use, but they would not hold. After that they went in search of paper clips.

Despite all his cricket, and despite his hectic social life, Tim had in the end (very much in the end) completed a remarkable amount of revision for his A-levels. Over the two years he had learned how to write logical and convincing essays, so that Anna Jo found that talking through topics with Tim helped to clarify them, although revising with him was a non-starter. To Tim the argument of an essay was the most important part rather than the factual content, and his ideas often helped her to produce a more logically argued piece of work than she otherwise would have written. On the other hand, Tim's technique of tackling an essay was to take copious notes from what he read, so that he was by no means unaware of the factual basis of the argument he was developing. This meant that for Tim, essay writing could be rather slow (this seems to have been particularly the case in history, where he became absorbed in the Tudors and Stuarts) and inevitably resulted in late submission. Nevertheless, by the time the exams came round, he knew a great deal and was competent in expressing it.

There was never any doubt that geography was Tim's core subject. According to Nick, who took the geography A-level exams with him, Tim desperately wanted to do well in them. The physical geography exam, however, appeared to be a disaster, since none of the questions they had revised appeared on the paper. Those, however, like Nick and Tim who had earlier done Oxford Entrance, could fall back on the work they had done for that. They had all revised lowland and upland glacial features. The geography master had worked out for them that questions came in cycles and the fact that the previous year there had been a question on the influence of time on glaciation seemed to guarantee that it would not come up this year. In fact, however, essentially the same question came up.

Another was a map question, which was also a great shock. As soon as they entered the hall, they could see that on every desk there was a map, which turned out to be a map of Scotland. Everyone freaked out, by Nick's account. They had to describe features with reference to the map and all the names were in Gaelic, apart from anything else. Tim did a question on soils, which no one was very good at, and the anticipated question on plate tectonics failed to materialise.

When the results were announced, Tim found he had an A in his beloved geography, a B in history and a C in English.

He was pleased with himself for that. Unaccountably, however, he failed the S-level papers he took in both geography and history, and though nothing really hinged on these, it was a minor blow to his pride. The A in geography A-level was what counted, and it was worth celebrating.

That summer, providence had smiled on Tim.

15 Zimbabwe

On 27 August 1987 Tim wrote in a letter to Anna Jo from the Hwange Safari Lodge in Zimbabwe: 'Once arriving at the Safari Lodge it has not taken me long to say that this place is unbelievably amazing. On Wednesday we spent from mid-morning until 4 p.m. soaking up the sun and swimming in an open pool all in front of an amazing view down a shallow valley where many wild animals also are soaking up the sun and drinking water.' He saw 'giraffes, zebra, buffalo, elephants, waterhogs, a leopard, monkeys and many varieties of birds plus other more obscurely-pronounced species. We have seen both dawn and dusk and felt surprisingly cold in the process.'

Here was Tim enjoying himself in the kind of climate and open spaces he was used to from Australia, Tim the hedonist, Tim with his mind and body receptive to the best and most beautiful things the world had to offer, Tim full of the joy of living. But the serious Tim was also much exercised on this MCS 1st XI tour of Zimbabwe, both as captain of the team and as an observer of the social and political situation in a Third World African country.

The bald statistics of their match results show that they played six matches, lost five and won one. These results were disappointing and Tim certainly believed that some of the lost matches could have been saved. The age-range of the players was wide - from 14 to 18 - the environment required a good deal of adjusting to, one of the players missed two matches because of illness, and bad luck also had a role. Tim's abilities as a captain were stretched, and it required great efforts to maintain morale. The team was accompanied by two masters from the school, Neil and Mike, both of whom were young and had good rapport with the team. The results also suggest that the performance of the team was improving as they went on, and indeed it was the final match that they won.

In their first match against Christian Brothers' College in Bulawayo they were soundly defeated. They started well by taking five wickets for 76, but then, in Tim's words, 'any loose bowling was severely despatched and in their 50 overs they ended up with a respectable 230 runs, having not wildly impressed me with their cricket skills. That score to me seemed a reasonable target and we started quite well but soon got tied down to accurate bowling. I was caught behind for 34 and it was not long before batsmen were out quickly trying to accelerate the run-rate. After tea we lost our last four wickets for 0 runs (yes zero) and ended up all out for 76 [the official statistics say 74]. We had hardly done ourselves justice!' Tim called a team meeting later that night in an effort to raise morale, and told Anna Jo that he surprisingly had a quite optimistic view for the subsequent matches.

He then turned to another aspect about the match that concerned him: 'only one thing: 9 of their players were WHITE and it seems this is likely to be the case in the majority of matches but not all. The main reason for this is not segregation or anything, just a slow process in trying to encourage the black majority to really take up the game. I hear you saying "I'm not surprised"! However, the fact remains, we have come over here to play predominantly whites in a country where they are in an élitist very small minority. To me this is a big blow but something I'm coming to terms with.'

On the way back to the hotel after this match Tim, Rupert and Christian were given a lift in the same car. During the drive an incident happened. I have accounts of it from all three of them, which differed slightly in detail but agreed both in the essentials of what took place and in their own reactions to it. According to Christian, the three of them could not believe how the driver spoke about a black truck driver - possibly a merchant - who was holding them up. In the words of Rupert: 'As we were driving along, a woman pulled out in front of us. She was not a confident driver, but she was slow and safe. Our driver said: "bloody blacks, why not keep them off the road?". We all then went quiet, though the conversation later picked up again. Then back in the hotel, Tim said "Did you hear what he said?". Tim's view was that the whites were out-numbered but thought they could do what they wanted.'

Tim's account of the incident to Anna Jo was uninhibited: 'In the evening after the match we had our first real chance to talk to and meet white Zimbabweans. We were somewhat stunned, Chris, Rupert and I, when one of their players driving us to the hotel called an old slow truck holding us up "bloody niggers". As the evening went on, despite a serious piss-up with a few of their players, this comment summed up their attitude to life in Zimbabwe.' He went on to express his irritation about the continuous praise of South Africa he was hearing, and concluded: 'Not only did the majority of our views have to be put to one side to remain sociably friendly, but in the morning, I (like others) began to realise what a boring and incredibly conservative group the white Zimbabweans are. They seemed very narrow-minded which disappointed me, yet was certainly worthwhile experiencing. Hopefully we will see a more appealing side in days to come.'

It seems that they did see a more appealing aspect of white Zimbabweans, because their next match was against a colliers' side at Hwange. They lost this match too, but more narrowly, by a difference of 24 runs. Unusually Tim fielded rather than kept, and placing himself as number six in the batting order was dismissed for 11 before he had properly settled in to the crease. Nevertheless, the lower batting order did well, and they were within sight of victory. Everyone agreed that the colliers were far easier to get on with than the people they had met at Bulawayo. They were of course, grown men. One of them, Pierre, was a huge man who batted without gloves. After the match the beer flowed, they sang tour songs together and had a riotous evening.

Quite late that evening they went by coach to the Spray View Hotel at Victoria Falls. Over two days of sightseeing, they experienced the size and thunder of the Falls, walked above the Falls past Livingstone's statue down to the bridge that marks the border between Zimbabwe and Zambia, visited a crocodile ranch where they could handle baby crocs, saw the traditional craft village which showed how the local thatched huts were made, went on a cruise down the Zambesi at sunset (Tim waxed lyrical about this) and saw a display of traditional African dancing. There was no cricket and they were able to sunbathe by the hotel pool.

Tim sent a postcard of the Victoria Falls to his principal geography master, which read: 'I could tell you that Vic Falls were formed because of an uplift of basaltic lava in the Jurassic period causing the Zambesi to flood over the top, but what I'm sure would interest you more would be that we have spent the first week eating, drinking, soaking up the sun and occasionally playing cricket! Unfortunately, in the field we have lost both of our warm up matches to unsensational opposition. Next week in Harare we hope to do better. Thanks for a rewarding and enjoyable couple of years.'

From Victoria they returned to Harare and played, successively, Prince Edward School, St George's, Eaglesvale and Plumtree, all as part of a schools cricket festival. There were 16 teams in the festival, including the Bulawayo team they had played earlier. Prince Edward School was the most racially mixed of the teams they played, with perhaps three Asians and two Africans included. MCS began well against this team and were 99 for 2, but then were all out for 165 and allowed Prince Edward to surpass that score for a loss of six wickets.

The next team, St George's, was from what is apparently the most prestigious school in Zimbabwe, the team was all white, and the umpiring appeared to be so biased against the visiting team that they received an apology. Here Tim scored 53, the team was in a strong position at 98 for 2, but after the umpire had got rid of most of the middle field MCS was 130 for 10 against St George's 177 for 8 in their 55 overs. According to Steve, Tim following this match was a great ambassador and made good friends among the St George's players. This was apparently at Rosalina's night club, of which more later.

The penultimate match was against Eaglesvale, who beat them by the narrowest of margins (8 runs), Tim making 48. And finally against Plumtree, which is close to the Botswana border, they won by 5 runs (191 against 186). Here Tim distinguished himself with a 70. Mike's view was that Tim had a better technique than any of the Zimbabwean players, but they were able to put away the ball every time, which was why they ultimately had the edge. For the team as a whole, pitches were much faster than in England and less receptive to spin, so that at first especially they were too cautious and scored

Story of Tim

much too slowly. The MCS team attracted a great deal of attention at the festival, no doubt because it was the only English team. Christian had to drop out of the last game because of a back injury. He remembers the sun going down and feeling that it was like a flashback. The teams they had played before were rooting for them and people were saying: 'if Tim's still in you'll do OK'. After the Plumtree match Tim was asked by Neil to make a speech at the final presentation. The speech, it seems, impressed their hosts with its maturity and poise.

The day after their final match Tim especially was delighted to be able to watch New South Wales play Zimbabwe. The Australians were on the top of their form, and a New South Wales batsman, Mark Waugh, hit five sixes and a four in the final over.

One aspect of their time back in Harare for the festival which caused some apprehension in advance was that the team members were all billeted in families. None of these families were black, for reasons which they guessed at, but the first of two families where Tim was billeted lived in a quite rural area and was by no means well off. Rupert, who shared this accommodation with Tim for two nights, recalls that when they went to bed they were told to bar the doors to stop animals entering at night, and to leave the windows closed so that they should not be disturbed by cockerels crowing early in the morning. They ignored this second piece of advice and sure enough, around dawn they were woken by loud crowing. Tim woke up in disbelief at his surroundings and asked 'Where am I?'. Later Tim stayed with a second family, who were very kind to him, and corresponded after he had returned to England.

It was remarkable that all the boys, including the younger ones, were shocked by the instances of racism they encountered among sections of the white community. Some of this has been related already. Neil and Mike were invited to lunch at an exclusive club in Harare, where it was soon obvious that this was not a place for blacks, unless serving behind the bar. They saw a white ordering toast from a black behind the counter. The black told him: 'Sorry, master, toast is off'. The white replied: 'What do you mean, you black shit?'. At the same place a white woman used similar language when she thought a black had short-changed her, though as it turned out, he had given her the correct change. Elsewhere they witnessed a group of drunk rugby players strip off and bathe in a fountain. A white man shouted at them: 'You shouldn't do that in front of women and in front of blacks. The blacks will be laughing at you'.

These experiences changed Neil's views on the issue of sporting ties with South Africa and he could also well understand why Mugabe wanted to scrap reserved white seats in Parliament. On the other hand everyone was struck by the warmth of the welcome and hospitality the team had received, largely from whites.

Apart from the issue of racism, the team saw ample evidence of economic difficulties, with many basic items unavailable in the shops including spare parts for motor vehicles. They noticed that the tyres on some of the vehicles they travelled in would have been illegal in Britain. While they were actually in Zimbabwe a law came into force making the wearing of seatbelts compulsory. Hardly anybody, however, had seatbelts fitted, and they appeared to be virtually unobtainable. Apparently no sporting equipment was manufactured in Zimbabwe, so that they received offers - in unconvertible currency - for much of their cricket gear. They were granted vivid first hand evidence of the gap in facilities and standard of living between the countryside and the city in an African country, exacerbated at the time they were there by a severe drought around Bulawayo.

Neil tried to find out why so few blacks played cricket, and concluded that the principal reasons were: lack of background in cricket for Africans; poor, though improved, facilities in schools; a marked preference for rugby and soccer (both now dominated by blacks rather than whites); the outlay in time and money required to play cricket, and possibly a perception that it was the 'colonialists' sport'.

And so to Rosalina's (possibly Rosalind's) night club in Harare, where the older members of the team repaired in the evening after the match against St George's, together with members of the St George's team. Jon remembers as an unforgettable experience celebrating the victory in their final match over Plumtree with a second visit to Rosalina's: 'Everyone was on a high, we were fairly plastered on beer, which is cheap in Zimbabwe, and we were looking forward to going home. Tim was a terrible dancer, but at the disco he was in the middle of the floor picked out by the spotlight which lit up his hair, and he just said to me "Isn't life marvellous?"

'The Zimbabweans drink beer from bottles without using glasses, and we discovered that if you bang one bottle onto another, bubbles will rise and soon the beer will come out explosively. So I banged the bottle I was holding onto the one in Tim's hand. Because it was very wet on the outside, Tim lost his grip on it and it smashed onto the floor. At this point we thought it wise to make an exit.'

If Zimbabwe was an absorbing experience, travel there and back absorbed both time and nervous energy. The team was booked on a package tour by Balkan Airways, which was operated by Bulgaria, and which included the stay at Victoria Falls as part of the package. As Tim rather graphically explained to Anna Jo, the flight to Harare fell short of his normal expectations of comfort. As soon as he entered the plane he changed into track suit and flip flops (thongs to Australians), whereas the others stayed in jackets and ties. Apart from food which members of the team compared to army rations, there was an interminable wait at Sofia Airport, followed by stops at Malta and Lagos. At Lagos Steve enterprisingly exchanged a nearly empty bottle of deodorant for a can of coke, and they duly noted that the two toilets boasted running water and electric light between them, but neither had both.

When they stopped at Sofia again on the return journey, they encountered what Neil described as the world's least organised place. They had to go upstairs from the plane to collect boarding passes, standing in a seemingly endless queue. The airport had evidently been recently computerised, and its efficiency had suffered accordingly. Several boarding passes were spat out of the machine, and then some more, but when Neil examined the second lot he found that these were for a flight in the evening. It became clear that the 170 seat flight had been overbooked by some 95 names.

Neil insisted that they all travel on the same morning flight, and refused to accept the six passes which had been issued for the flight in the evening. They waited for about an hour saying they would not accept the evening passes, and then after another half hour the woman official came up with two more passes. After two hours more she produced another, and half an hour later the remaining three. Unsure that passes would guarantee them seats, they made sure they were at the front of the queue *en bloc*, and that everyone ran to the plane from the lumbering bus which took them across the tarmac. When takeoff was delayed, he issued instructions that nobody should leave his seat, as the stewardesses were walking up and down looking for spare seats and even brought extra ones into service. There were no overhead lockers, only roof racks as on a bus or train.

The expedition thus gave them some little insight into the Second World as well as the Third.

16 Dairy and Bicycles

After returning from Zimbabwe Tim began the serious business of preparing for his 'year off', that period of transition between school and university when he could be what the Japanese like to call a *rōnin* or 'leaderless samurai'. Being Tim this required an all-out effort to make sure that he could pack in as many experiences as possible. To fulfil that aim also meant first earning some money to pay for it all.

Through an employment agency he found work in the County Dairies in Kidlington, where he along with other leaderless samurai worked long hours carrying boxes of milk, cream, orange juice, yoghurt and other products, stacking and unstacking the cold store, and performing similar tasks. Tim with his sporting interests was extremely fit, but at least in the early stages he came home exhausted after such intensive manual labour.

Organisation of the year off in part revolved around the anticipated presence of his two childhood friends from Australia, Stephen and Rob, who having also finished school, were seeing the world (as young Australians are so fond of doing) before going into tertiary education. The three of them planned to make a tour of several countries in Western Europe in October and November, using interrail passes. Already in September Stephen had arrived, and stayed with us for a period while working with Tim at the Dairy. Stephen had serious artistic talent and was planning to go to art school back in Australia. Normally he said very little, though he was a lively observer of everything that went on. One evening Stephen and I watched the Oxford philosopher Anthony Kenny on TV discussing medieval philosophers. He developed an interesting argument about how medieval logicians had been familiar with arguments which had only surfaced again in the twentieth century. Stephen's whole being seemed to light up, and we began discussing philosophy, with informed and animated arguments from Stephen. He was less interested in a programme on Madagascan lemurs later in the evening.

Rob arrived later, shortly before they were due to depart for the Continent, having travelled on a double-decker bus through India and the Middle East, on a 'Top Deck' tour with a party of Australians. They even crossed a part of Iran despite the Iran-Iraq war, and in that country the women on the party were required to dress with Islamic modesty. Rob assumed an 'Ocker' manner, and much later gave us a slide show including an account of the bus trip, which had us rolling with laughter for its 'Crocodile Dundee' approach to foreign parts. But the manner overlay an impressive intelligence and a strong sense of practicalities, especially financial ones. Rob was good at bringing wayward personalities down to earth.

We ourselves were away a good deal during this period. While Tim was in Zimbabwe, Audrey and I were on holiday in France, in late September and early October I was back in Japan and Korea, and in November once again in Tokyo for a conference. Every time I returned home, there were new exploits to be told, and every time the household seemed to be differently composed, as various friends were staying or had just left.

One relatively long-term visitor was a friend and workmate of Tim's brother Rupert, who was called Jonathan. He had been on the same arboricultural course in Surrey as Rupert, and was now working as a tree surgeon with Rupert and his boss in the Cotswolds. His stay in our house remains vivid in the memory. Unlike Rupert ('Skip' to Jonathan), for whom a tie was as exotic as a top hat, Jonathan cared deeply about his personal appearance, dressed stylishly in a blazer and fashionable shirts, and Audrey observed from the washing basket that his *underwear* was bought at Austin Reed. He regularly made hour-long telephone calls to his Swedish girlfriend in Stockholm, and when he left he had to make a contribution to our telephone bill in excess of £400.

Jonathan had applied for a work permit to work in Sweden, and this required a fair amount of bureaucracy including an interview in London. The day before the interview Tim had borrowed his car with his permission but omitted to put any petrol in it. As a result, when Jonathan set out for Oxford to catch the train to London, he ran out of petrol just beyond the village, missed the train to London, was not granted an interview for another fortnight and had to postpone his departure for Sweden. When he next saw Tim, who was overwhelmed by guilt, he put to him that there was a little problem relating to petrol, but found annoyance with Tim could only briefly be sustained. 'You can't really be cross with Tim, can you?' he said.

Michael, from Pressed Steel Fisher, once took Tim and Stephen to a pub after a cricket match. After rounds had been bought and consumed, the two of them were told it was their turn to buy a round. They emptied their pockets onto the bar and found they had 43p and 37p respectively. Michael had earlier discovered that Tim believed in purchasing petrol in amounts of £1 and at the last possible moment. His philosophy on cars was that everything was fine so long as the cassette deck worked.

During 1987, however, problems with cars were rather frequent. The Mini had died at the beginning of the year, and Rupert had bought for a small sum an ancient Morris Traveller, which was hardly a paragon of reliability. Car crises were frequent, and Tim would find he needed to make last minute emergency arrangements for transport to matches and other appointments. He and Stephen reverted to pedal power in travelling the three miles to the County Dairies and back. One day in early September, however, I fetched Tim and his bike from Kidlington after he had put in a day at the Dairies which began at 6.00 a.m. and ended at 8.00 p.m.

I myself was cycling to and from work (ten miles each way) rather often during this summer. One day in September my rear tyre suffered a puncture on the way home through Yarnton, not far out of Oxford. I tried to telephone home for a lift but the phone was always engaged, however many times I tried to ring. Back home I found Tim had tied it up, as usual, making phone calls to his friends. It took me two hours to walk pushing the bicycle and carrying a heavy briefcase. No doubt I found some words to say to Tim on the subject of the telephone.

17 Europe - Interrail

Stephen, Rob and Tim set out on their travels on 12 October, crossing the English Channel from Dover to Calais. The day before Tim was due to depart there was a great crisis, because the automatic cash dispenser at his bank in Woodstock inexplicably 'swallowed' his cash card, and the bank was already closed. Somehow or other, Audrey was able to sort the problem out, and he was able to retrieve his cash card. Almost throughout the trip, Tim wrote a diary which ran to 75 pages of an A5 notebook, and also wrote detailed letters to Anna Jo, so their exploits are well documented.

They experienced parts of France, West Germany, Austria, Italy, Spain and Holland (Tim also crossed Switzerland and Belgium), saw museums, lazed on beaches, explored 'crumblies' (Rob's word), met a variety of people, both locals and travellers like themselves, saw the insides of railway carriages and hostelries, drank the wine (occasionally to excess), shivered on shuttered stations in the middle of the night, renewed their childhood friendship and cemented it into one of young adulthood.

There was one piece of business that Tim was determined to carry out on this trip, namely to find a ski resort in a German-speaking area where he could work in the winter as a *Kuchengehilferer* or an *Abwascher*. His plan was to spend the skiing season working in a ski lodge, return home in the spring of 1988, and then fly to Australia for a month's return to his homeland before coming back to Oxford in time for the cricket season, and to captain the Colts.

They therefore decided to head straight for Austria, so that Tim could explore job possibilities in ski resorts as quickly as possible. They took a train to Strasbourg, arriving at 12.30 in the morning, but found there that their connection to Salzburg did not run on that day of the week and they had a long cold wait for the Orient Express, which passed through at 4.24 in the morning. At first they donned extra jumpers, took their backpacks and set out to explore the town. Rather than ladies carrying baskets of baguettes, they encountered only ladies 'offering their services' and drug pushers in alleyways, so they returned to the station where there were no seats and no heating, only a drunken derelict who sang German ballads at the top of his voice. As Tim confided to his diary: 'most definitely a soul searching time - waking up to reality'.

When the train arrived it was so crowded that it took them 45 minutes to make their way to the sleeping car, but they then managed four hours sleep and arrived in Salzburg in the middle of the morning. On a warm sunny day in that lovely city they sat eating ice cream in the Mozart Platz. The next day, after catching up on sleep at the Youth Hostel, Tim spent 36 Austrian schillings on a 50-minute bus ride to Berchtesgaden over the border in Germany. He was, however, too late to visit the *Arbeitsamt* and most hotels told him there were no jobs. The one hotel that did not simply say 'no' told him to come back in the evening when the manager was home, but this was after the bus left which he needed to catch back to Salzburg.

That evening, the three of them went by train to Kitzbühel where they spent the night. Tim was much impressed by this resort, but he spent the next day frustratingly trudging from hotel to hotel and speaking to some by phone. In most cases the replies he received were either *'keine Ausländer'* or *'zu spät'* ('no matee' as he translated it). In the evening Stephen and Rob went off to Vienna as Tim had one appointment in Kitzbühel to make the next morning. He later wrote in his diary: 'Had quite a promising conversation with the landlady. She spoke good English and after giving her my CV, reference etc, she said she couldn't offer me work immediately but asked if I could return after 1 November, when her final places would be arranged.' He wrote the news as a postscript in a letter to Anna Jo and said he was feeling more optimistic.

He in turn took the train to Innsbruck, where the three of them had agreed to rendezvous in the evening. He explored the central city ('clean and very old') and while waiting for his friends on the railway station was reading a Colin Dexter whodunnit. Then: 'Continued my latest fascination - watching people walking by. Who do they remind me of back in

England? What sort of character do I think they have? What were they doing last night? etc.'. Gregarious Tim. Stephen and Rob arrived by train from Vienna at 10.00 p.m., where they had been 'looking at crumblies'. At 1.42 in the morning they caught a train heading for Florence.

Tim's diary entry for 17 October (Day 6) reads as follows:
'My first day ever in Italy.

'Backpacked our way around the streets of Florence for over an hour in muggy warm conditions looking for a cheap place to stay the night.

'A bustling city, overcrowded, too much traffic in tiny narrow streets, very easy to get flustered. City was also dirty and smelt rotten in some places.

'Eventually found a Pension for £7.50 a night (44,000 lire for 3 persons). Dropped off packs and began to wander around. Florence suddenly grew on me. No longer concerned about car horns, smells, overcrowdedness. In fact these just added to the wonderful brash atmosphere of the place + the Italians themselves.

'Generally much more laid back people than Austrians. Also got the feeling by the old decrepit housing, that housing was not what mattered to these people. It was more what sort of car they drove, what wonderfully stylish clothes they wore or where they ate out - winter fashions had seemed to have hit the street despite it being a gorgeous hot afternoon after the haze had lifted in the morning.

'The main buildings and squares had so much character of the past and today. The main river, although dirty added to the splendour of the Italian lifestyle. Minute by minute, the whole place and especially its people grew on me.

'Had an afternoon siesta in hotel then bought cheap potent 1½ litre bottle of wine which succeeded in making me, and company, somewhat drunk. The relationship between the three of us grows closer each day and no subject remains beyond the bounds of discussion.

'In the evening, we wandered around the lit streets with many shops still open. The locals had changed their clothes from smart original casual to evening wear of pure quality. Nibbled at slices of pizza and drank more beer as the laid back wonderful atmosphere was soaked up. What a place to remember. So much more lively, one feels, than the cities of England. And one thing's for sure. I've never tasted such fantastic ice cream!'

Later that day they caught a train to Pisa and climbed the leaning tower, where Tim was affected by his phobia about heights. Rather than staying in Pisa they continued their journey to Siena, where they found the youth hostel after a long walk in the dark and met an Australian who had been travelling for six months. I may have persuaded them to go to Siena, as I had sung its praises to Tim having landed there as a hitchhiker on *my* first trip to Italy in 1956. Tim described it accurately and noted in his diary how they 'lay down on the cobbles like many others eating a huge supermarket lunch and sunning ourselves in the clear blue sky we imagined how long it must have taken to build the belltower as we gazed up at it. (more photos)'

Their capacity to do without sleep is remarkable, because they left Siena on a mid-afternoon train heading for Naples, where they arrived at 9.45 in the evening. They were intending to catch a local train from Naples to a remote town or village and sleep their first night under the stars. They thus caught a train along the coast to Salerno but around the Bay of Naples round to Salerno found everywhere was built up. They therefore took a snap decision - to catch an overnight train to Sicily, leaving at 2.15 a.m. On this journey they were awoken by a train inspector in the middle of the night telling them that they had to change carriages since their carriage had been detached from the main train. They 'scrambled in little more than boxer shorts plus open pack + sleeping bag on to new carriage which was crowded. Achieved possibly two hours sleep on this occasion'.

Their train entered the railway station of Reggio di Calabria (on the straits overlooking Sicily) at 7.30 in the morning. About an hour before Stephen had seen from the train a small town called Nicotera which had good secluded coves and beaches. They caught a train back there and abandoned the idea of crossing to Sicily.

At Nicotera they 'backpacked up a steep road to the main village 3km away... and backpacked down to a nearby cove having to do some very steep traversing down a mountain with packs on our backs - a hair-raising experience. The ground was loose and slipped away from your feet. I dropped my pack and saw it tumble down about 10 metres - luckily no damage'. They found a place on the beach to camp, where 'the sounds of waves crashing, birds flying and chirping and the odd fishing boat dominated over any other sounds', and they prepared to spend a couple of days relaxing. That night they ate ravioli with tomato sauce and drank between them a two-litre bottle of palatable white wine. Next morning they 'woke at dawn with the bright sun breaking through the marram grass and the noise of the waves crashing on the pebbles'. In the village of Nicotera Tim noted that there were smart seafront buildings 'but in the backstreets the backwardness of southern Italy was clearly evident. Communist graffiti, unfinished building which looked [as if] it had run out of capital'.

After Nicotera they caught a northbound train and spent the next night at the youth hostel at Sorrento, which Tim noted was excellently cheap at L6000 per night and gave them congenial English, Australian and American company. They went out for a 'proper meal', having a pizza, a bottle of wine and an ice cream. Next morning they wandered round Pompeii wondering what happened when the volcano blew, experiencing evidence of 'the lifestyle the people led from gent to slave', and noting 'stepping stones which used to be Zebra crossings', as well as 'some wonderful Roman paintings'.

In Rome, their next stop, they were pounced on by a tout who persuaded them to stay at what turned out to be a dingy and, by their standards, expensive pension, where they objected to paying a thousand lire extra in government tax, and expressed their disgust by adding further graffiti to the mouldy peeling wallpaper of their room. That evening they drank too much, as Tim rather graphically confided in his diary. This did not prevent them doing some of the Roman crumblies the next day and looking with awe at St Peter's, the Vatican Museum and especially the Sistine Chapel.

'Evening - Saturday night too good to miss, spent most time at the fountain de Trevee (spelling?) [i.e. Fontana di Trevi] and on these steps in a big square listened to buskers, devoured ice cream etc and had good philosophical discussions with Steve. What a great person he is!

'Caught night train to Venice at 12.00 midnight.'

In Venice it was overcast and they found too many tourists. They enjoyed themselves but came to the conclusion that it needed more money than they had to spend, so late the next evening they took a crowded overnight train to Nice, arriving at 9.30 in the morning. They admired the stylishness of Nice, but Tim observed that at one spot they found themselves 'surrounded by the dealing point for all drug-pushers on the Côte d'Azur'. He noted, however, that French MacDonalds appeared to be far more clean and civilised than those in Oxford, or even Austria.

Once again they took a night train, this time to Barcelona. It was crowded and noisy so that they had little sleep. On arrival they found a youth hostel where they could leave their packs, and after finding their bearings, followed Stephen to the Picasso museum. Tim declared to his diary: 'Never have I been so incapsulated [sic] in artwork before. Steve, of course, lapped up one of his favourite artists'.

Back at the youth hostel they talked to many Australians and Canadians, had long-awaited showers and were able to wash their clothes. They were pleased to find that it seemed possible to live in Spain on £10 a day. The next day they visited other museums and saw sights in Barcelona, ending up at the Café José, whose reputation for cheapness in various guide books made it a haven for many 'fellow travellers who condescended [sic] on the place'.

In fact they made many friends among the 'fellow travellers', but Tim found that he had mixed feelings about some Americans he met. On the one hand, during their last day in Barcelona, he 'met a young American couple who were very talkative and interesting. For the first time I've met more than just a few people who are very anti-Reagan... Maybe Americans are not so bad after all, or at least young American travellers'. But on the crowded train that night to Madrid, there were 'three... American girls studying in London for a term. They seemed to have money to burn or their fathers did. They had flown to Geneva, travelled down to Nice and then on to Madrid all in the space of a week and were then catching the train back to London, having supposedly 'done' Europe. What was worse... they soon moved to a first class carriage because of the crowdedness! I know Spanish trains are the worst in Europe but these people seemed to expect to be wrapped in cotton wool! I have images of these rich girls turning into the middle-aged American who comes over on a package coach deal to England, staring out the window of the coach without actually getting in amongst what makes a country a country - its people'.

They did not stop in Madrid, but went on through to Toledo, where they stayed in a marvellous youth hostel located in a castle, saw the sights and met more Australians as well as a Californian working for a protest organisation against the CIA. Next afternoon they returned to Madrid, found good accommodation for 1000 pesetas each, and prepared to celebrate Rob's and Anna Jo's birthdays, both of which fell on the following day. We shall pass over Tim's diary description of what happened that evening, except to note that he had to field complaints of noise from the hotelier, both of them communicating in their common second language, German.

Next afternoon they headed for Segovia, two hours north of Madrid, where they stayed at the youth hostel and once again met a variety of 'fellow travellers'. After settling in they 'headed into the old town to see the sun set over the crimson red rooves *[sic]* lighting the numerous churches, castle and aqueduct up into an amazing splendour'. They ate the *'menu de la casa'* at the cheapest restaurant they could find (600 pesetas) and had 'Castilian soup to start with (a concoction of everything and anything including a whole fried egg), trout as main course and caramel flan for pudding'. Tim stopped off for a Spanish hot chocolate on the way back. Among the 'fellow travellers' was a Sydney University graduate in medicine called Christine who, when Tim was beginning a letter to Anna Jo, took the writing paper off him and wrote a page of her own about Segovia and then assured Anna Jo that Tim had not quite fallen into true Spanish decadence (except for the odd hot chocolate) since he even let strange females write his letters for him. Tim then completed the letter.

Meeting Australians, and others from the 'new world', as well as travelling with Rob and Stephen, awakened in Tim a renewed enthusiasm for the country he was born in, and at about this time he wrote in his diary: 'I've got the impression that nearly all Australians travelling that I have met, begin to realise the beauty of their own country when they are away from it. Endless memories of holiday times on the coast, holidays in the mountains and the bush and life on the north shore of Sydney'.

I took a brief telephone call from Tim in Segovia; he wanted to find out Anna Jo's local telephone code, so that he could ring her on her birthday. He also rang the hotel in Kitzbühel, but found the hotelier still did not know whether she would be able to employ him in the winter. He thought the prospects were still good, but as a precaution, decided to split from Rob and Stephen at this point and travel back to Austria to look for work at St Anton and at Davos in Switzerland. It would mean he would miss Paris, but he would meet them again in Amsterdam.

There was, however, still Avila to visit, where the sun unusually failed to shine, and Burgos, where they stayed the night. The following day Tim's train arrived at Irun ten minutes after the night sleeper had left for Nice, so after contemplating various unattractive alternatives, Tim ended up travelling with his companions overnight to Paris, where he could catch the train to Zurich and be in St Anton by the next evening. To his diary he sang the praises of French railways by contrast with those in Spain.

In Paris he saw from *The Times* that Australia's cricketers had reached the final of the World Cup in India, but did not have enough francs at that point to buy the paper and find out who had scored the runs. During the long train journey to St Anton across France and Switzerland, he read most of *Anna Karenina* which he had exchanged with one of the Australian girls in Spain for his Colin Dexter. Who is to say that it was not a fair exchange?

His first encounter in St Anton was hardly encouraging. Going from the station to the Bahnhof cafeteria recommended by his ski-jobs guide, he was told 'go back home' and 'not another ski bum!'. But in the intense cold of a November evening in the Alps he soon found a place to stay with a hot shower and food - important as he had not eaten all day. He also found that three Australians from Sydney, Tony, Jason and Andrew, were at the same place, also looking for winter work, and pessimistic about the chances of finding it. Tim was persuaded the next morning (after bread and jam and hot chocolate) to postpone job-hunting until the afternoon, and to accompany the Australians up the mountain behind the town. They 'set off up into the sunshine and climbed up above the valley gaining some magnificent views'. He rejoiced that it exercised his calf muscles and his heart: 'it was great to break out into a sweat and to smell the alpine air - unforgettable'.

When he started knocking on doors, he found the locals much more friendly than they had been at Kitzbühel, and he was gradually developing more confidence with his German. At the fourth place he tried, the Gasthof Freisleben on the edge of town, he struck lucky and was hired for the whole of the ski season as a kitchen helper. He returned to the Tyroler Frieden where he was staying in a triumphant mood. The others were pleased for him. They ate goulash soup at the 'Barni' (Bahnhof), and along with some Swedish ski bums they played ten pin bowling with some locals. As he told the diary: 'I could hardly get to sleep as I thought of spending a winter in such a fantastic resort'.

He had been told that he would have to find his own accommodation, so he decided to spend the weekend at St Anton with the others, looking for somewhere to stay for the season and doing some more walking. 'The Kitzbühel job would be going out of the window.' The next day, however, he found that a single room at a price he was likely to be able to afford was practically impossible to discover, and commented to his diary: 'Maybe the Kitzbühel job was still worth pursuing.' He also wrote that the others thought it was crazy for an employer to expect his workers to find accommodation in a millionaires' paradise. The next morning he went for another invigorating mountain walk with Tony, who impressed Tim with his experience in travelling and his interest in windsurfing, mountain bike riding, surfing, cross country running and downhill skiing. Let Tim take over the description of this walk without interruptions from me:

'We stopped to have our mandarins about half way up the huge mountain and looked over the valley through the trees to this awesome glacier carved into the mountain-side above St Jacob. After a twenty minute relaxation period in the glary sunshine (sunglasses a must and that's without the reflection of the snow!), we headed back down the mountain leisurely walking back through the village while all the locals went to the active Sunday Church service. This Austrian village offered not only some of the best skiing supposedly in Europe but remained traditionally Austrian in its ways.'

In the afternoon Tim returned to the Gasthof Freisleben where 'in the pleasant surroundings of the bar-restaurant, I could speak to [Herr Freisleben] who had his Chef hat on and who had been busily cooking for the lunchtime visitors'. He was told that he would be given accommodation after all, and that after initial training he would probably be moved to the hotelier's other restaurant, in Pettneu, six kilometres down the valley, where he could have a room. He would work 10 a.m. - 2 p.m. at the Gasthof Freisleben, and in the evenings, but at the restaurant in Pettneu he would only work in the evenings, being able to ski all day long. The pay was 8,000 schillings a month (about £400), which Tim agreed was a fantastic wage considering that food and board were thrown in. He would start work on 14 December.

That night - Sunday - he had another goulash soup and beer with the Aussies and Swedes, 'before finishing with a game of chess before a fairly early night. More dreaming about those off-piste black runs!'.

After some discussion with his future employer by phone about work permits and other matters, he 'said "goodbye until I return" to all the Aussies and, after having a conversation with a mad drunk claiming all Austrians were Nazis, in the railway station, I caught the train to Basel arriving at 11.35 p.m'. Then he continued:

'I was lucky enough, after a couple of hours, to get an empty carriage once getting on the Amsterdam train. I did, however, have to chain my pack to the seat, as well as myself, because of a suspicious man who kept coming in and out of the carriage. Not a great night's sleep.'

He woke up to find that the train was approaching, not Amsterdam, but Calais, two countries away. Like many others he had been in the wrong carriage. With an American in the same predicament, he took a train from Calais to Lille, 'then waited hours for a train to Antwerp, and then caught the train up to Amsterdam'.

The diary ends at that point. In fact he successfully met up with Rob and Stephen in Amsterdam, at the last of four pre-arranged meeting times. The next day they returned home.

The laconic Stephen, finding later that Tim's diary stopped with his arrival in Amsterdam, uttered the single word: 'good'.

I have noted earlier that there was something of the chameleon about Tim: in Oxford he would easily slip into imitating the characteristics of his close friends: when he was with Jon he would become one of the hearties, but when he was with Pete he would engage in theoretical disputation about politics. In the dynamics of friendship this made him an important link between them, although there was the odd occasion when he failed to manage this successfully.

Something of the same process could be seen in his relations with Rob and Stephen, both of whom he had known since early childhood and whose personalities he understood well. Tim himself believed that his own personality lay somewhere between that of Stephen: intellectual, philosophical and otherworldly; and that of Rob: practical, sharp as nails and inclined towards commercial values. Once again Tim the chameleon found he could identify with either of them, and in their travels around Europe this linking role helped the three of them relate together in a relaxed and deepening friendship.

18 One of Life's Little Things

Back home Tim resumed work at the County Dairies with Stephen for a while, though he soon took a job on the check-out at Littlewood's supermarket in Oxford. He became quite proficient as a 'check-out chick', but his friends would file through with items from which they had removed the price tags, so as to confuse him.

Tim's capacity for exuberance comes out in Philippa's account of a dinner which she, together with Anna Jo, Tim and Jon had at an Oxford restaurant on 5 December. Tim was extremely frustrated because they had to wait for 45 minutes before they could sit down and he was eager to see all his 'mates' in the Wheatsheaf. Eventually, however, they were allotted a table and sat down. When it came to ordering it was agreed that Tim and Jon would share a side salad and so would Anna Jo and Philippa. The waitress asked what dressing they would prefer and this led to 'major probs' (as Tim would say). Jon wanted Thousand Island and Tim was adamant that he wanted French dressing. When Tim realised that Jon would not change his mind he tried to explain to the waitress that they wanted a bowl of side salad, but could she arrange it so that half of it was covered in French dressing and the other half Thousand Island. The waitress thought that he was joking but Tim was extremely serious about it.

When Anna Jo and Philippa were asked they suddenly realised that it would be better if Jon and Philippa shared one with Thousand Island and Tim and Anna Jo had one with French dressing. The poor waitress had to change her order again! Tim just looked at them in a completely confused way and was very worried that he was not going to get his French dressing. He was delighted though when he saw a WHOLE bowl of salad with French dressing and Philippa is not sure how much of it Anna Jo actually ate. Tim found it quite difficult to eat all of his pizza because he had 'pigged out' on

One of Life's Little Things

the salad. But they enjoyed a memorable evening.

Jon remembers visiting Tim at the Littlewoods check-out and being told by him that that night they would be eating out at the restaurant, which Jon was unsure he could afford, being short of money at that point.

The next day, Sunday, they had tickets for a Suzanne Vega concert at Wembley Stadium, which was an event they had been looking forward to for some weeks. Suzanne Vega with her haunting voice and sometimes agonised lyrics appealed to these intense 18 year-olds who could perceive, at times acutely, that life had its tragic side. Similarly Tim's English master found that it was common for the boys he taught to think that they would not enjoy Hardy, but then to be tremendously taken up with his novels when they read them. He thought it was Hardy's gloomy fatalistic latter-day romanticism that seemed to appeal.

On Sunday Tim, Anna Jo, Jon and his girlfriend Caroline drove our aging Volvo Estate to Princes Risborough to pick up Philippa and her sister. In retrospect, the car, which we had bought second hand after moving to Oxford from Australia nearly six years before, was approaching the end of its useful life. As they were driving into London they had forewarning of trouble when the footbrake started interfering with the radio which finally conked out. Then suddenly, at traffic lights, the engine died. Jon pushed the Volvo along the dual carriageway. The oil light was on so Tim suggested they put some oil into the engine. This they did and the car started again. About half a mile from Wembley the engine died again, so Jon and Tim told the girls to walk to the concert, arranging that they should meet afterwards at the stadium car park where they hoped to put the car.

The two of them went to look for a house with a phone. At the first house they went to the door was answered by a Rastafarian with dreadlocks. Tim told him they would pay for the phone, and they gave him about £1. Jon told Tim to go to the concert while he waited for the AA man, so Tim only missed about the first 15 minutes. When the AA man came he could not find anything wrong with the car, but thought there might be a problem with the battery. Jon therefore drove the car in the direction of Wembley car park, but unfortunately took the wrong turning and started driving in the wrong direction. This might have been a problem with their arrangements for meeting if the car had died elsewhere than at the car park, but eventually he found his way to the car park and just as he arrived the engine died once again. At last he was able to go to the concert but had missed all but the last ten minutes, consisting mainly of encores, and was understandably rather annoyed.

When they all returned to the car, Tim suggested that this time they call the RAC since we were members and Tim thought that maybe the RAC would accept him as a member as one of the family. In fact, the RAC man made him join, at the cost of some £38, for which Philippa wrote a cheque. He asked the RAC man the same question several times in a different format. Tim had Anna Jo's scarf tied around his neck, as it was by this time 11.30 p.m. on a cold December night, and he was in such a good mood, despite everything. The RAC man phoned a garage and was able to tell them that they would fix the alternator, which turned out to be the cause of the problem. When the garage man arrived, however, he towed the car away so they had to phone Philippa's mother at Princes Risborough to come and fetch them. She kindly arrived sometime after one o'clock in the morning.

In all this crisis Tim said: 'don't worry, it's one of life's little things'.

The weekend of the Suzanne Vega concert was also the weekend when Audrey held the annual exhibition and sale of her pottery in the workshop at our house in Wootton. It was a few days before Tim was due to leave for Austria, with various arrangements still to be made, and ski clothes to be bought after shopping around carefully to check prices. Arrangements included, as it would emerge, the necessity of fetching the car from a garage in an obscure part of London.

Audrey would sometimes become exasperated with the chaos and loose ends which Tim tended to leave behind him. But as she later reflected, he had a very caring, generous and magnetic personality, and despite his intense need to fill every moment, and the fact that he was always running late, he would pop into the pottery (usually to borrow the car or some money) and say 'that's a great pot, Mum'. Audrey's pottery was the topic of conversation at dinner one evening, and Tim was concerned and upset that she worked such long hours for such little reward. He had a quiet but supreme self-confidence and would say, if she couldn't decide what to do about something: 'Go for it, Mum!'.

He saw that there was little point in being too much deterred by the little obstacles of life when there was so much to play for.

19 Mega-Party

On the evening of 11 December 1987 a thick, dirty yellow asthma-inducing fog descended on Oxfordshire, such as I had not experienced since my schooldays in the Midlands during and after the Second World War before the clean air acts. On one occasion then in Birmingham, my parents, attempting to navigate in minimal visibility by following the line of the curb, suddenly found a brick wall looming immediately ahead of the car. On closer investigation, they realised they had driven right into a hotel car park.

That night in Oxfordshire I deliberately stayed late at work, having many things to catch up with and knowing that back home, the chances of doing any work were nil. It was probably 10.30 or 11 o'clock before I drove out of Oxford north along the Woodstock Road, through the almost invisible town of Woodstock and out towards Wootton. The whole journey was slow and laborious through the fog, with street lights making the eeriest of light patterns into the murk, and reminding me of my childhood in Birmingham long ago.

When, however, I turned off the A34 onto the 'top road' above Wootton, a road lacking any central markings or curbs, but just leading between fields over the rise of a gentle hill - a road which normally made me settle into a mood of relaxation and contentment - suddenly I found myself disoriented. The car headlights, even when dipped, reflected off the fog straight back into my eyes, I had little idea where the road ended and the grass verge began, or which side of the road the car was taking. The fog seeped into the car and made me worried about my breathing as I am susceptible to asthma. Gradually, painfully, I found my way to the turn into the village, down to the River Glyme and along it for a distance, then over the bridge and up the corkscrew hill through the village and at last back home.

Once through the door I walked into a quite different world.

Mega-Party

The party, mega-party to commemorate Tim's departure for Austria the next morning, was in full mega-decibel mega-throbbing flow. Tim and Anna Jo had invited about 40 of their friends to live it up, and live it up was what they were doing with great abandon. I have long since forgotten the quantities of beer, or the numbers of bottles of wine that were consumed that evening, but a timely advertisement from a firm of cleaners led to them being summoned by Audrey the next day to shampoo the living room carpet, clean several curtains and generally remove the ample evidence of spilled beer as well as doing something about the pervading smell of nicotine. At one point in the small hours Tim gently told me that I should not go into the living room, but I saw that several gentlemen of the party were stripped to their underpants and performing some outrageous dance.

I also cannot now easily remember whom I talked to, except that for more than an hour, maybe closer to two hours, I sat with Stephen, the normally quietly observant and untalkative Australian 'mad philosophic scientist', as Rob once called him on a birthday greeting to Anna Jo from Spain, as we earnestly debated the relevance of contemporary theories about astronomy to the philosophical basis of one's understanding of existence. There was nothing untalkative about Stephen that evening, but much that was penetrating and sane.

There was no question of anybody trying to go home that night, and Nick actually missed the party because the fog was so bad the people who were driving him turned back on the way to Wootton from Woodstock. When they grew weary, people bedded down in sleeping bags all over the house, which became an obstacle course of prone bodies. Somebody told us that at another similar party the head of household had ordered girls upstairs and boys downstairs, then stationed the family dog on the stairs to keep order. We lacked a dog, however, so no such policing was attempted.

Audrey and I went to bed at about 3.30 in the morning, after picking our way between sleeping bundles. I remember perfunctorily saying goodbye and wishing luck to Tim, who had to leave at around five o'clock to be driven to Oxford to catch a bus to Heathrow for a plane to Zurich, from where he would go on to St Anton by bus. Audrey and I would see him

Story of Tim

in early January when we joined him for a week's skiing at St Anton, and Anna Jo was booked to go on Boxing Day. There seemed no need for any ceremonial parting. I was actually asleep when he left. Audrey got up to say goodbye and he yelled up the stairs "Bye!'. Anna Jo said, 'Tim, that's out of order. Go and give her a kiss'. And that was what he did.

As he prepared to leave, he turned the light on in the living room and said, 'Right, I'm off then'. The response was, 'Turn the light off!'. Tim's car, in the memory of his friends, was always full of coats, bags and other paraphernalia, which tended to fall out when he opened the car door. Angus remembers how, at five in the morning of 12 December, Tim went off in his moon boots, and there was Tim, Anna Jo, Philippa and Jon crowded into a small car together with all his gear. It was typical of Tim.

In deference to Tim's partiality to ice cream he was given, along with other going away presents, *The Cool Handbook*.

20 Austria

Tim began work at the Gasthof Freisleben as scheduled on Monday 14 December. Much of the following account of the next few days is based on the recollections of a fellow Australian, Paul, who was working with him in the kitchens of the Gasthof, and of Michael, a German with whom he skied.

According to Paul the Freislebens were very nice people, and in general St Anton employers were much better than those at Kitzbühel, where there was an oversupply of Australian and other ski-bums looking for work. When Tim arrived - a few days after Paul - he quickly 'took control' of the kitchen. Appropriately enough, Tim was mainly responsible for making ice cream and salad garnishes, while Paul was on salads. Tim also organised the hot chocolate, which they drank every morning. In many places this would not have been allowed, but Herr Freisleben was very lenient about this kind of thing. Tim also performed a variety of other kitchen duties, including washing up.

When Paul arrived, he thought he would be the only 'traveller' working in the Gasthof kitchen, but he was soon joined by Tim, a Yugoslav called Nedelko, a German called Willi and a Swede called Mats, who arrived rather later. Tim was given a room at the Gasthof to share with the German, Willi, who, it turned out, both smoked heavily and snored loudly. These problems were so bad from Tim's point of view that he took his bedding onto the landing and slept there. Even the girls in the adjoining room objected to the snoring. Tim, indeed, told Audrey about Willi in the course of a phone call, and said that he had confronted him with the phrase: '*Willi, wir haben ein Problem*'.

During the first week, they spent most of their time outside work making arrangements for the hire or purchase of ski gear. The weather was so bad that week, with rain some days, that there was no point in attempting to ski, although they did ski a little. They managed to make an arrangement with the ski shop to buy ski equipment at a 40 per cent discount, and they were also able to keep their skis in a locker at the same shop, an important concession since the Gasthof Freisleben was some way out of town. Tim also spent time looking for somewhere for Anna Jo to stay, and succeeded in finding a room for her down in the town. They rang each other more or less nightly. When she phoned him, she would have to go through a switch, and when after three minutes she was still not connected, she would ring off and ring again. When the line was finally connected to Tim, he would bellow 'don't ring off!!'. Once, when she was talking to him on the phone, she heard a great roar, and Tim said, 'the Aussies have arrived!'. She had the impression that during the first week he was not able to explore the night spots of St Anton because he was working evenings, but he had been for beers somewhere in the mountains with friends.

Sunday 20 December was Tim's nineteenth birthday. I spoke to him on the phone. I do not have an exact memory of what we said but I remember clearly the sound of his voice, which was cheerful and animated. He had opened the presents we had all given him to take with him, and told Audrey that Herr Freisleben had stood him a beer, which had surprised and pleased him.

The next morning he went skiing (not for the first time). On one of the runs he met a West German of his own age, Michael, who was on leave from national service in the *Bundeswehr*. They shared a chair on the Schindlergrat-Bahn and Tim asked him if he spoke English. When they reached the top Michael left him because he thought Tim was with his friends and waiting for them. About half an hour later they met again on the ski-lift and agreed to ski together. Tim had left his friends because they went down pistes he did not like.

They stayed together the whole day, and Tim told Michael about his interrailing holiday, how he found the job at St Anton and his plans for the future. He said he wanted to teach Anna Jo to ski when she visited him in a couple of weeks. When Michael asked if she could already ski, he said no but he hoped she would learn quickly as she was good at sports, did a lot of riding and had a good sense of balance. He also spoke of his plans to go to Australia where he was born, and that the ticket was already paid for.

When Michael told him he had been to the USA and liked it very much, Tim said that he might visit his sister Jane in the States in September, before going to Oxford University to read geography. He also suggested Michael should not miss Oxford if he went to England in the summer, because it was such a lovely town.

Conditions in the mountains were beautiful, the afternoon went very fast, and when Tim had to leave, Michael asked him if they might ski together again. Since he had a car, he suggested that they should go to Zürs or Lech where Tim could not easily go without a car. It was impossible to ski together on the Tuesday because Tim had to go to Landeck, the nearest town down the valley east towards Innsbruck, in order to obtain a work permit, and to have a medical, as required for work in kitchens. He also had to help shift a load of wood at the Gasthof. They therefore agreed to meet on Wednesday morning, 23 December, in St Anton.

On Tuesday Tim duly passed his medical and obtained a work permit. In the evening Anna Jo and he spoke on the phone but he forgot to mention that he had met Michael or their plans for the next day.

On Wednesday morning, Michael saw him when he was walking from the Gasthof Freisleben to the sports shop where they had agreed to meet and where Tim kept his ski gear. Michael gave him a lift to the car park, but Tim told him that he could not go to Zürs because he had to start work at noon back at the Gasthof. At the car park Tim realised that he had forgotten the key to his locker, so they drove to the Gasthof again to fetch it. Michael thus learned where Tim worked. They then proposed to go to ski at the Rendl-Bahn, but there was not enough snow there. They therefore had to go to the main St Anton skiing area with the Valluga-Bahn, the Valluga being the name of the highest mountain of the range behind St Anton. They skied again several times on the Schindlergrat-Bahn, and later went down to the Alpe Rauz, where they had already skied once or twice on the Monday.

When they went up the lift again they saw that a person had skied right under the lift, where no run was marked (though it is sometimes so marked, as the ski run map shows). Tim suggested they should try that run because the snow was better there, so they followed the track and met the main run down to Alpe Rauz in its lower part just above the last steep bit before it flattened. They skied down, stopping occasionally to admire the view, and when it began to flatten out Michael skied ahead of Tim to the lift station, which was round a corner to the left, and waited there for him.

Tim, however, did not appear, so after a while Michael went back to the corner at the bottom of the run, perhaps 50 to 100 metres away. He saw no sign of Tim but also no sign of anything peculiar and so he skied back to the lift and asked the man who checked the tickets whether he had seen Tim. He had not and so he went back round the corner again. As he still could not see anything odd and as it was now nearly twelve, he thought that maybe somehow they had passed each other without noticing and that Tim was either waiting for him at the top or had not waited because he was now in a hurry. He went up the lift but he was not there either, and he waited another five minutes before he skied down again to see if he could see him anywhere. As he could not, he convinced himself that everything was all right and skied until the late afternoon.

When he drove home he stopped at the Gasthof Freisleben (he only knew that Tim worked there because of the incident of Tim forgetting his locker key) because he wanted to ask Tim for his name and address, which he still did not know. He went in and asked whether a tall fair-haired English boy worked there. The owner's wife asked him whether he was talking about the one who had suffered a fatal accident that morning.

The accident happened close to the bottom of the run, where the piste was not steep at all and about 20 metres wide. To its right there was a creek bed, about two metres deep, and it was into this creek bed that Tim fell down a 45° slope from the edge of the piste. He struck his head on a rock and was killed instantly. The snow conditions were rather poor and there was not enough snow to cover the rocks in the creek bed (as there would have been, no doubt, later in the season), but the snow on the piste seems to have been adequate enough, there was no ice, the sun was shining and visibility was good. Why an experienced skier such as Tim should have fallen so disastrously at that place and in such relatively easy conditions remains unresolved and there were no witnesses. In Michael's opinion he had been skiing with all due care and not taking risks, and it was a run they had done several times already.

The reason Michael could not find him was that he was out of sight in the creek bed. Nevertheless another skier did find him quite quickly, because with the fall his skis had come off and were still at the edge of the piste, and the emergency services were alerted. Nothing could be done for him.

Michael went to the local police station at Klösterle to find out what had happened, and there he met the mayor who said that the accident was completely inexplicable to him. He spent a miserable evening on his own and drove back home to Germany the next day. His father later rang the police station from their home and was told such other details as were by then available.

About seven months later, in the summer, Anna Jo, Audrey and I found Tim's sunglasses, and a broken stock, at the place where he had died. We collected some mountain flowers and put them there for him.

Epilogue

Tim's story ends at that point, and the reader will probably wish to put the book down without reading any further. The following is intended as some very brief reflections on the aftermath of Tim's death and the problems of this kind of bereavement. But first I need to mention a curious episode that occurred a few weeks earlier.

One night, perhaps in November, the doorbell rang insistently in the middle of the night, when we were at the deepest level of sleep. Roused eventually, I went downstairs and found a young policeman and a policewoman at the door. They told me that our car door was open and asked me to check that it had not been broken into. I realised that I must have left it open bringing some shopping into the house in the evening. After I locked the car, they were satisfied and went away.

The night of 23 December is embedded in my memory like a series of photographic plates permanently stuck in the brain. At around 11 p.m., I was looking at old photos with Kate and her new boyfriend Mike, who had arrived from Australia, by way of a holiday in France, just over 24 hours previously. Audrey had gone to bed, while Rupert and his girlfriend Maggy were watching an old black and white TV set in his room separate from the house. The doorbell rang briefly, a bit late I thought, but there was nothing so strange about that. Two middle-aged policemen were at the door asking whether this was Glym Cottage. When I said yes they asked if they could come inside.

My immediate thought was that they had come to tell me once again that something was wrong with the car, but there was an element in their manner which put me on my guard. I had only the briefest of moments to think like this because they told me straightaway that Tim had been involved in an accident. I said something about how serious was it and one of them, after the slightest hesitation, obviously trying to gauge

Epilogue

how I was likely to react, told me that he had been killed. My immediate reaction was to turn away from the front door and walk towards the living room, but one of the policemen grabbed me round the waist thinking I might faint, obviously standard practice. I said, 'I'm OK', he let go and I went to the living room.

The mind moves fast in circumstances like this. My first thought, as I walked through the kitchen was: 'well, we shan't be going skiing in Austria after all'. Extraordinary. Then as I walked along the corridor to the living room I worked out what I would say to Kate and Mike. For the first time I felt my legs beginning to give way under me, but I made an effort and recovered from this, and came out with the standard formula: 'you will have to prepare yourselves for a shock...'.

After discovering some basic details about what had happened from the policemen, I went around the house to tell the others, beginning each time with the same formula. I think in retrospect I have never seen anything so sad as the reactions of everyone to what I had to tell them. We rang Anna Jo's parents, but she was already in bed and her father decided to tell her in the morning. In fact she had been expecting a phone call from Tim that evening, and when none came she wondered vaguely if she had upset him in some way. Kate rang Jane in the States where she and Russell were now living and they decided to come over as soon as they could find a flight. We did not sleep that night.

I shall spare the reader any systematic description of the next few days and weeks, except to say that many people were very kind to us; but rather attempt to make a few tentative generalisations from our experience. At the same time, it should be remembered that I am in no sense a bereavement counsellor, and that this should be taken simply as personal reflections on one family's experience.

Here, however, I need to mention a fact that I have deliberately withheld until now: in 1970 Audrey's sister Julia died in a drowning accident in Australia. In other words we had been through it all before, and knew something of what to expect. On the other hand we felt doubly targeted, and tempted to fall into moods of acute bitterness for that reason.

The first point is that although a sudden death such as Tim's is something which a family experiences in common, every individual member's reaction will vary slightly. Each member is in a different relationship with the person who died and may have other reasons for feeling somewhat differently. Audrey initially reacted as though he had still been a child and she was desperately concerned to find out whether he had experienced any pain in the accident (it later became as clear as it could be that he had not). For a while I was obsessed by the fact that I had not said goodbye to him at the party properly but had allowed him to breeze out of my life with scarcely an acknowledgement. We remembered him differently, too: Kate and Jane had not seen him for two years or more and thus thought of him as much younger than he actually was when he died. Rupert felt his death with especial acuteness, because, though there was the usual sibling rivalry to some extent in earlier teenage years, in the last year or two they had become extremely close as the complementary nature of their talents and personalities became evident.

Secondly, I think that every family reacts differently. In our case, we felt a need to investigate Tim - his life as well as his death - bring him metaphorically to life by finding out more about how he had interacted with his friends, to write about him and talk about him, however painful it might sometimes be. We felt we needed to visit where he had died, painful again though that might be, and indeed was. Psychologically, we could not let his memory die, and photographs were not enough. Part of this may be a need for catharsis, part for greater understanding of one's own feelings, but part also may stem from a perfectly rational desire to tell the world about somebody who should be interesting to read about, but cannot any longer tell the world about himself. On the other hand, this has to be a more or less finite process; the dead person must not become a permanent obsession, but rather a proud and tender and, in a sense, living set of memories. We opened a fund in memory of him, which was generously subscribed, and earmarked sums for a charity in Africa, and for school and cricket purposes.

Thirdly, as any book on the subject will tell you, there are stages of bereavement. They are not fixed stages, common to everybody, nor are they more than amorphously defined. They will also greatly differ depending on the acuteness with which the loss is felt in the first place. From our experience, the first stage is a curious numbness, almost lack of feeling, no doubt medically associated with shock. Hence perhaps my own strange instant reaction to note that we would not be going skiing. There is an analogy to what happens in physical injury. This, however, does not last long - a few hours at most - and is succeeded by the most overwhelming feeling of grief in which crying and a mind that races all over the place in confusion, seem characteristic. The symptoms are quite physical; I felt as though I was dragging myself round with a lump of concrete tied to my leg.

After that, the rites of passage associated with death may well describe the boundaries between stages: Tim's funeral in the village church in which his school chaplain eloquently used cricket as a metaphor for his life; later a memorial service at his school, in which his friends participated, reading extracts from his European diary, in which representatives of his cricket clubs, successive schools etc., spoke about him, and his favourite music, including Suzanne Vega, was played. The next stage for us was a gradual return to something like normality, but with many ups and downs, still much overt grieving and - an important activity - much letter writing. The placing of a stone on his grave in the churchyard was a sort of stage, nearly a year later.

And then there is a period of years, in which a gradual distance from the trauma is achieved and the pain becomes less acute (though without ever disappearing); yet on the other hand you are aware that the person who died is receding further away into the past. Tim is stuck at 19: what would he be like now? There can be no answer to that except in the imagination and it requires increasing effort to keep him 'alive' in the mind's eye. Certain events, like a wedding or a birth, will even so bring the old feelings flooding back: why is Tim not here at Rupert and Maggy's wedding, or at Kate and Mike's wedding? Why is he not here to see his new niece and nephew?

Fourthly, particularly in the early stages, families who go through an experience like ours need a good deal of help, often on very practical matters. In circumstances like these one simply is not thinking straight, for reasons of shock and lack of sleep. We became extremely emotional because the local bank, having heard of his death, refused to accept a cheque he had left with Audrey, though the issue was later sorted out satisfactorily. I personally found I could not take sleeping pills (fortunately, perhaps), and an inability to sleep was a real problem for a time. Andrew, a friend who spoke fluent German, rescued me from trying to make sense on the telephone with my bits and pieces of German to the Klösterle police station, negotiated with various bureaucratic agencies in Austria and translated our letters into German. We were helped enormously by many people; but some things one needs to do oneself, for both practical and psychological reasons. It is important not to fall into a habit of dependence, though it is also crucial not to reject help and bottle one's feelings away.

One of the most emotional stages was when we received his belongings back from Austria. His ski boots became almost taboo objects, and the unbelievably beautiful blue ski jacket which Tim had bought with such pride before he left was returned undamaged but soaked in blood. The dry cleaners would not touch it because of fear of AIDS, but gave Audrey detailed instructions on how to clean it, which she did. Searching through his things became a psychological process of trying to bring him back. A medical friend and his wife accompanied us when we saw Tim's body in an undertaker's dingy back room after it had been brought back from Austria. We could hardly have gone through that on our own. Even so, there was a certain wry humour in thinking that Tim, who complained that a room for £5.00 a night in Spain was expensive, should have ended up in an even less salubrious establishment in death. He would probably have preferred it to some ghastly 'funeral parlour' with ornate and irrelevant fittings.

My fifth point is that many people, quite understandably, do not really know how to approach the bereaved, or how to handle them on either a short-term or long-term basis. Death is, after all, the 'last taboo', and all of us are in some measure scared and disoriented by it. The conventions are supposed to help with this problem, but it seems to me they often get in the way of a sensible and sensitive reaction. In my view the worst way of dealing with the recently bereaved is to act as though nothing had happened. Still worse, even, is the attempt

Epilogue

to change the subject when the bereaved makes reference to some aspect of their loss. People said to me once or twice: 'I just didn't want to remind you of it', to which my unstated reply was 'I don't need reminding of it; I think of it all the time': (not strictly true, but it was the way I felt). A very few people went to the opposite extreme and wanted to talk about it to excess. But that is in general a good fault, especially in the earlier stages.

Even a long time after the event, there may well be a need to talk things over with a sympathetic listener. The trick is just to let the bereaved person talk and seem interested, not try to steer the conversation onto other things. The bereaved has a problem of much complexity to deal with over the long term, which is how to re-orientate his or her life to deal with the absence of the person who has died. He or she may well need help with this, though again the caveat needs to be entered that people are different, and may have different needs. Some people also simply do not realise how long the process of adjustment can take. I was quite taken aback to be asked, some six months after Tim died: 'Have you got over the death of your son yet?' My immediate response was (not unstated, this time): 'I don't think you ever *get over* it'.

We received an avalanche of letters and cards from all over the world after Tim died. For weeks, reading them was a breakfast ritual. Some, quite reasonably, were brief, formal or perfunctory. Others were deeply felt, carefully thought out and enormously comforting. Wryly, we became connoisseurs of condolence letters, and found ourselves discussing their merits quite objectively, and not without humour. We received many letters from Japanese friends, many (which I translated) written in Japanese. Most of them were marvellously sensitive letters, and Anna Jo, who had not experienced Japanese before, was fascinated. The following Christmas, in Australia, Kate, Jane, Audrey and I sat in the Botanic Gardens of Victoria in the shade of a big old eucalypt and read through many of the letters again. I went for a long walk round the lake and imagined I saw Tim as some kind of effervescence from the surface of the lake. It was a strange and powerful experience.

Another important, but I think often overlooked, point is that it is not only the family that is bereaved. Tim's close friends told us graphically how intense the effect of Tim's death upon them was, who in most cases had never experienced death (except, perhaps, of an elderly relative). Anna Jo said to me that she found it hard to believe that somebody could simply disappear. In the event they counselled and comforted each other, meeting frequently over Christmas and New Year of 1987-8 and continuing to keep in touch (with each other and with us) over the years.

We discovered something that we had not really suspected before, that there is a community of the bereaved, or rather, a community of the similarly bereaved. I am not talking of organisations such as Compassionate Friends, though they are a more organised form of the same thing, perhaps. Through a mutual friend we received a helpful letter from a family in South Wales who had lost a son in an accident. Kate, in a dentist's waiting room in Melbourne, found an article in a women's magazine written by the headmistress of a school in New Zealand whose son had been killed by a vehicle and who had found solace in writing about him and about his death. Thus began a most sympathetic correspondence between us. Audrey sees regularly in Oxford two mothers who have had similar experiences to herself and feels a particular bond with another who lives further away, whose son also died in a skiing accident. I personally think there is a danger in over-institutionalising such contacts, though some people may need this.

Finally, I hope I will be forgiven for saying a very little about the philosophical problems of our kind of experience. This is a strictly personal approach, and I expect many to disagree with me. After Tim died, one or two people put to us some variant of the proposition that his death should be seen as an expression of God's purpose for the world, and we should not expect to comprehend this since 'God moves in mysterious ways'. Though these comments were kindly and sincerely meant, I found (and still find) myself in complete disagreement. I cannot believe in a world where there is a supernatural entity that behaves like some kind of urban terrorist slaughtering people's loved ones and causing misery to those that remain for reasons that are unknowable. Some Christians have told me that these are no longer contemporary Christian notions, and I hope that they are not. From a different perspective, a person we met in Austria explained Tim's death to us in terms of the workings of *Schicksal* (fate). This, however, is surely little more than a panglossian term analogous to 'explaining' the nature of water by its wateriness.

Rather, what led to Tim's death was the coming together of a virtual infinity of chains of circumstances, culminating in the final miscalculation of stance, direction, speed, or whatever, that sent him hurtling into the creek bed. At any point beforehand the fatal connection of chains could have been averted. He might have gone down the same piste more slowly, or at a different angle, he might have gone on a different piste, there might have been more snow, he might have had to work that morning, he might have taken the job at Kitzbühel instead of St Anton, he might have gone straight to university instead of taking a year off, we might have stayed in Australia instead of returning to Britain. It seems characteristic of human nature that one explores these 'might have beens', and even experiences guilt or attributes blame to oneself or to others who appear responsible for fixing in place particular links in the chains. Clearly, however, without intention there is at the very least diminished responsibility, so that it is a doubly fruitless exercise: it is morally unjustified and it cannot bring him back to life. What I personally see no evidence for, and strongly believe to be a redundant hypothesis, is the notion that behind these chains of causality there is some extra force operating which does exhibit intention, and somehow, beyond the reach of human understanding, manipulates the causality for its own ends.

Speaking again very personally, one strong reaction I experienced was a sense of disillusionment about just deserts. This led to a danger of falling into an attitude of bitterness towards the world, but I think I recognised the dangers in this and consciously resisted it. Nevertheless, Tim's death was extraordinarily disillusioning in a generalised way. In no sense had he deserved his death: it was hugely unjust. I realised that subconsciously, and of course naively, I must have accepted a view of human affairs which held that in the end people received their just deserts; the good went on to great things and the bad were found out. I understood that in broad terms I had assumed this to be the case even though my conscious mind knew it was often false, and indeed that human history includes many atrocious exceptions to the rule. Tim's sudden, utterly senseless death, dashed this subconscious expectation. I no longer believed in the rule. It has been hard to come to terms again with reality as a result.

This is not, however, to say that these events do not have a pattern and meaning; Tim's life to me has a very important meaning, which it has been my intention in this book to convey. But it is a meaning in terms of our own understanding, the patterns we as human beings with our own peculiar nature place upon reality. It is also a meaning in terms of the understanding which Tim himself was developing of the world and his place in it, of the life he was mapping out for himself and his capacity to inspire others. All I am saying, perhaps, is that Tim meant something that is intrinsically valuable, and that that something is worth telling.

Before he went to Austria, Tim bought me for Christmas an Arthur Rackham print. It shows a fantastic sea creature cleaving the waves of a stormy grey-green sea. The creature is part sea-snake, part horse, with horse-like head and flowing mane, but more sea-snake than horse. To its neck, which surges high out of the waves, clings a child, hair blowing way out in the wind, legs tangled in seaweed, face shining with the incomparable adventure of being alive.

Poems

IN THOSE ORDINARY TIMES BEFORE THE NEWS
In those ordinary times before the news
I did not hear the doorbell ringing
2.35 a.m.
Persistently ringing and I go downstairs
find the police ringing
'The door of your Volvo open and a window'
I say I was very fast asleep
and somebody must have left it open
'Is that all it was?' they ask,
'Box of pottery in the back'
'All there is to it,' I say
Thank them and take off my shoes
Go back to bed.

In the nearly Christmas time we look at photos
Old family photos of the early sixties
Kate a baby and Japan and friends
And people hard to recognise so young
11.15 p.m.
This time I hear the doorbell ringing
This time not persistent waking me
Slowly out of a deep sleep
But short and sharp and unambiguous
Or so it seems in retrospect
Two policemen 'looking for Glym Cottage'
'Here,' I say, 'then may we come inside?'
There is something sinister about their kind quiet voices
Not the usual matter of fact
'Skiing accident in Austria' ' your son has been involved'
I formulate a question, complex and not yet understanding
Like 'what degree of seriousness?'
Almost I might be probing some student essay
Hesitating for a mega-second, then
'Killed' they said.

Story of Tim

Policemen you have unpacked
My guts and chucked them at the wall to mingle
With Tim's spilled brains.
But that is hardly fair. These are
kindly fatherly men who hold me to stop me falling
But I am not fainting yet but formulating
Some set phrase 'You'll have to
Prepare yourself for a shock' and this
Repeated several times around the house to anguish
'Not fair' you say, but what is fair about
A fair-haired golden boy hurled against a rock in Austria?
'No witnesses' and 'foul play not suspected' then
There is nobody for me to hate that did it
An inert rock that lay in wait for him for aeons
For him to slip so slightly on the icy path
And crush him out dead.

He would have died in good time
Another fifty years or even sixty
or less perhaps if holocaust came early
But he would have shone like Kohoutek's comet
Seen in the sunset from an aircraft window
In 1974 on the way to Tokyo, not announced
Over the intercom but seen by us together
As a light that attracted motivated inspired
Loved was loved cared was debonair happy
Careless of protocol but never hurtful
Had ambition would have reached the top
Not by climbing over others but by leading others
Lifting the spirits with a carefree gesture
Passionate in opinion and learning to understand
And scoring confident centuries on tended pitches
The comet has left into the far distance
Of the universe, and to satisfy the police
I have shut the car doors and secured the windows
And no more, no, nothing, to be said.

JAAS
29 December 1987

TRACK

Track the rucksacked wreckage in the block-strewn snow
Ink back the line from where it came

Trek from stop to starting down a life brought low
Turn round the order and rerun

Trick the broken molecules to think that it is light
Call down the figments of the mind

Trot through all experience to push away the night
Race round a track to no post passed

★

Some say
Life matters
But one life
Is small

★

Some also say
All life matters
So one life
Is all

★

Some say too
Life goes beyond
What we see
And feel

★

If it is so
To what other sense
Should our sense
Appeal?

Story of Tim

Truck the fractured life box to the tip of time
Break down the edifice we raised

Trudge now leaden-footed up the airless climb
Choke back what tears are left to cry.

JAAS
7 February 1988